The Spiritual Effects of Sex

By

Brandon Cash

2017

Cash Publishing LLC

Copyright 2017 Cash Publishing LLC

ISBN 978-0-578-67946-4

All rights reserved. No part of this publication may be produced, distributed or transmitted in any form or by any means, including photocopying, recording, or other electronic or mechanical methods, without the prior written permission of the author.

Unless otherwise indicated, Bible quotations are taken from The King James Bible. Royal Patented, Public Domain.

www.cashpublishingllc.com

Introduction

The bible mentions a word that some of you may not be aware of, that word is cleave.

Cleave- as an intransitive verb which means to adhere firmly and closely or loyally and unwaveringly (stick).

Cleave- as a transitive verb which means to divide by or as if by cutting blow (split).

Basically, cleave is either stick or split, in this book I will get into both meanings because the bible gives example of both definitions. I'm no expert but, I can share my input in some cases from past experiences. Since building my relationship with my Lord and Savior Jesus Christ, I have begun to understand the depths of strong holds we have begun to create while just freely having sex. Instead of doing it in the order of how God created it for us, we can now see how those strong holds have affected our lives. It has been revealed scientifically the effects of sex between you and your former partners; and throughout this book I will use evidence based off research or studies. I'm writing this book to shed some light in some dark areas and in return hoping to free people from whatever sexual stronghold they may have experienced or currently experiencing and restoring them back to God.

Table of Contents

How God designed it..5

Effects of having multiple partners..18

Beauty is vain 32

Masturbation 50

Homosexuality 59

Lesbianism...72

Pedophilia 79

Zoophilia..87

Necrophilia...96

Positions (Bonus Chapter)...102

Chapter 1
How God designed it:

Men are givers and women are receivers

God's original design, "Therefore, shall a man leave his father and his mother, and shall cleave unto his wife: and they shall be one flesh" (Genesis. 2:24). Based on this verse, it describes a structural order. Before the cleaving process were to take place, the man would have to find him a wife first. As it states in the bible, "Whoso findeth a wife findeth a good thing and obtain favor of the Lord" (Proverbs. 18:22). I haven't done this exactly in this order, but from my personal experience I'm writing this to show how it's properly done. Also, it states in the book of proverbs, "A virtuous woman is a crown to her husband: but she that maketh ashamed is as rottenness in his bones" (Proverbs. 12:4). When you get married you're going to receive one of the women described. I'm sure you would rather like to have the first verses the second. If you are already married or are deciding to get married, understanding the steps within the bible can make your marriage wonderful.

So, to find a suitable wife to share this wonderful experience with, DO NOT look solely on just her outward appearance. You would need to take into consideration her inwardly appearance which the bible also describes as her fruit. A biblical example, "But the Lord said until Samuel, look not on his countenance, or on the height of his stature; because I have refused him: for the Lord seeth not as man seeth: for man looketh on the outward appearance, but the Lord looketh on the heart" (1st Samuel 16:7). While reading this scripture, I received two precepts. First precept, "God is a spirit: and they that worship Him must worship Him in spirit and in truth' (John. 4:24). Second precept, "And the Lord said, my spirit shall not always strive with man, for that he also is flesh: yet his days shall be a hundred and twenty years" (Genesis. 6:3). Those two scriptures helped me to further understand the visual differences between God and man. God's vision is spiritual, it focuses on the potential of an individual, he sees further down the road. Man's vision is worldly, he sees things carnally at what is presented in front of him at that moment. Also, while reading both scriptures the first scripture declares who He is, being God; while the other scripture declares what He has said to further show his authority.

As you are seeking for your potential wife, search the heart through the word of God and it will guide you in the right direction on your quest. I'm going to give you a few examples from Proverbs 31 where it speaks in detail about a virtuous woman. Starting at verse 10 A question is asked, I believe to be a very important question for this day and age. It states, "Who can find a virtuous woman? For her price is far above rubies" (Proverbs. 31:10). Understand guys, you are not going to find someone that automatically fit into these examples without that woman wanting to strive for it. Also, notice she has a price just like the bride of Christ which have been brought with a price. The bible states, "For ye are brought with a price: therefore, glorify God in your body, and in your spirit, which are God's" (1st Corinthians. 6:20). Continuing, "The heart of her husband doth safely trust in her, so that he has no need of spoil" (Proverbs. 31:11). Truly understanding that verse will shows how blessed you are fellas when you have someone like that in your life. Quick precept, "Keep thy heart with all diligence; for out of it are the issue of life" (Proverbs. 4:23). This woman has her husband back no matter what. This woman won't just up and leave when things get tough, she's there through thick and thin which also shows her consistency. This man can come to her about anything and not have to worry if he married a talebearer. He knows that anything that he tells her is always between them. He doesn't have to worry about being exploited due to her being spiteful. He doesn't have to worry about a financial strategy in case of divorce, exit plan, or worry about having money to keep her around. He is very comfortable with her and is confident that choosing her was the right choice for him.

    This next verse illustrates that this woman having a vision and making an investment decision that will benefit her and her family. "She considereth a field, and buyeth it: with the fruit of her hands she planted a vineyard" (Proverbs. 31:16). I know currently it's not easy to purchase land in our time like it was back then. The verse in this illustration shows someone having a long-term vision (Like I was explaining earlier). You only see that kind of operation take place with wisdom from God. Her qualities continue, "She is not afraid of the snow for her household: for all her household are clothed with scarlet" (Proverbs. 31:21). She's thinking ahead for her household and preparing before it gets too late, realizing all could suffer. This is someone that goes out of her way to have the best for her family and is not a selfish person. Her motto is "if one looks good, we all looks good as a whole". Her entrepreneurship qualities, "She maketh fine linen, and selleth it; and delivereth girdles unto the merchant" (Proverbs. 31:24). Not only does she make her clothes which cuts expenses, she also sells them as well to bring in extra income. She's selling to the sellers, which make her a wholesaler, boss lady status. Owning your own business while being available for your family is a prime example of what this woman is about. An example of this practice in our modern day is, "Extreme couponing" like the TV show. You can get what your household needs, by paying little to nothing for it, while giving some away to the needy, and can also sell some for profit. Those are a few examples of biblical qualities to look for in your wife. If you are already married, pray for your wife to strive for those characteristics if she doesn't already have them.

    The bible describes a few women who had the characteristic of being a virtuous woman. Sarah, Abraham's wife being one and Esther being another; but, the story I have found to be interesting is the story of

Ruth. Ruth became a widow at an early age and instead of her going back to her family she decided to stay with her mother in law named Naomi. They moved back to Naomi's homeland and Ruth found work gleaning the field of Boaz after the reapers. She gained favor from Boaz due to the fact she remained loyal to her mother and law after the death of her husband. Boaz replied to Ruth, "The Lord recompense thy work, and a full reward be given thee of the Lord God of Israel, under whose wings thou art come to trust" (Ruth. 2:12). I believe this verse along with others foreshadows God's plan of grafting in the gentiles, because Ruth was a Moabite.

    Naomi noticed the favor from Boaz that was given to Ruth. Being an elder woman, Naomi gave wisdom to Ruth of how to present herself to her kindred Boaz (as a virtuous woman). Naomi suggested to Ruth, "Wash thyself therefore, and anoint thee, and put thy raiment upon thee, and get thee down to the floor: but make not thyself known unto the man, until he have done eating and drinking. And it shall be, when he lieth down, that thou shalt mark the place where he shall lie, and thou shalt go in, and uncover his feet, and lay thee down; and he will tell thee what thou shalt do. And she said unto her, all that thou sayest unto me I will do" (Ruth. 3:3-5). Looking at this advice that was given to Ruth, I began to see what is missing in our generation, advice from our elders to keep us as men and women, honorable and virtuous. The advice in our terms is, "freshen up", cover yourself spiritually as well, dress real nice and presentable, be noticeable but not thirsty for the guy. When he goes to bed, lift the cover off his feet, that was a sign during those times of letting a guy know you were interested in him. Ruth did everything that was told of her to do. While doing what was told, Ruth told Boaz that he was her nearest kinsman. Boaz replied to Ruth, "And now, my daughter, fear not; I will do to thee all that thou requirest: for all the city of my people doth know that thou art a virtuous woman" (Ruth. 3: 11). She ended up laying at his feet until the next morning and left before anyone would notice that she has been there.

Before they could get together, they had one more dilemma. There was a kinsman, that has more rights to Ruth than Boaz. Boaz had a sit down with the kinsman to offer the proposition for Ruth. The kinsman in question, didn't want Ruth due to the fact she was already once before someone else's wife. If he were to redeem her, it would be for someone else inheritance instead of his own. In other words, he wanted someone for himself that's a virgin and haven't belong to someone else. He offered her to Boaz like, "If you want her you can have her" (paraphrasing). Boaz accepted her and spoke life unto her where he compared her situation to Rachel, Leah, and Tamar the women helped build Israel and Judah as a nation. Boaz received her as his wife and she gave birth to Obed who is King David's grandfather.

HOW DOES CLEAVING HAPPEN

Cleaving as by definition to stick or to split which both can happen through sex. As you continue to read I'm going to give an example of cleaving as of splitting after sexual intercourse, but now I'm going to give the example of the meaning as to stick through sex. In Genesis, it talks about Jacob's daughter Dinah being defiled. In Genesis, it states, "And when Shechem the son of Humor the Hivite, prince of the country, saw her, he took her, and lay with her, and defiled her. And his soul clave unto Dinah the daughter of Jacob, and he loved the damsel, and spake kindly unto the damsel" (Genesis 34:2-3). That's what happens when your soul cleaves unto someone, you will catch feeling regarding that person or in other terms "whipped". I know in the past when you heard of soul ties, you may have heard that her soul attaches to yours and vice versa. According to what I have found in the bible it doesn't exactly work that way, let me further explain.

Notice in the scripture that was just read it stated that his soul clave unto her, it's a one-way process. Before I use a scenario, I want to use two verses from the book of Matthew. It states in Matthew, "When the unclean spirit is gone out of a man, he walketh through dry places, seeking rest, and findeth none. Then he saith, I will return into my house from whence I came out; and when he is come, he findeth it empty, swept, and garnished" (Matthew. 12:43-44). So, this illustration shows that a house is representing a human physical body or outer appearance. I have come across one more verse in the book of Job that proves my point. In Job, it states, "How much less in them that dwell in houses of clay, whose foundation is in the dust, which are crushed before the moth?" (Job. 4:19). When a guy buys a house (in this scenario the house would be a female), it is his after he purchased it and moves in to reside there. That's the same process spiritually when you are cleaving unto your wife. Why did I use a house to explain the female role in cleaving? The answer is in Genesis, "And the Lord said unto Noah, come thou and all thy house into the ark; for thee I have seen righteous before me in this generation" (Genesis. 7:1). What does Noah house consist of? Verse 7 of the same chapter gives us a clear description. Regarding Noah's house, "And Noah went in, and his sons, and his wife, and his sons' wives with him, into the ark, because of the waters of the flood" (Genesis. 7:7). This verse explained Noah and his wife through cleaving, his sons because they came from his seed, and their wives because his sons cleaved unto them.

    Now understanding how everything works, if you are married that make your job very important spiritually. Paul the apostle wrote, "The wife hath not power of her own body, but the husband: and likewise, also the husband hath not power of his body, but the wife" (1st Corinthians 7:4). After saying that, everyone that is in a marital relationship is responsible for each other for it to work. As a man, you wouldn't just reside in a ran down house, you would want to at least fix it and keep up with the maintenance. Also as a woman you wouldn't want anybody that present themselves any kind of way (dirty, drama, keeps an entourage of company) moving into your house to reside permanently.

In the next chapter, more details will be explained regarding having multiple partners pertaining to both men and women. I want to continue to expound on the word house as it pertains to Proverbs 14. The writer states, "Every wise woman buildeth her house: but the foolish plucketh it down with her hands" (Proverbs. 14:1). An example of her building can refer to her keeping herself virtuous, health wise and presence. Also, it can be her being a support system for her husband, speaking in him life and encouragement. Being a foolish person is a grown adult doing childish thing, playing kiddie games, "so to speak". Biblical example, "Foolishness is bound in the heart of a child; But the rod of correction shall drive it far from him" (Proverbs. 22:15). An example of a woman plucking down her house is destroying her body by drinking, smoking, defiling herself spiritually and sexually. Also, it can be is talking down to her husband, not only him but your household as well. As it also states in Proverbs, "Death and life are in the power of the tongue: and those that love it shall eat the fruit thereof" (Proverbs. 18:21). Hands in the bible usually means control, one example is in Genesis. Abram stated, "But Abram said unto Sarai, Behold, thy maid is in thy hand; do to her as it pleaseth thee. And when Sarai dealt hardly with her, she fled from her face" (Genesis. 16:6).

SHOWING THE SCIENTIFIC FACT OF SOUL TIES

"Researchers also have found that any man a woman has unprotected sex with also will permanently store their DNA with hers".

"Researchers have found DNA belonging to men (detected by the presence of Y chromosomes) in women. They could find these by taking blood samples from various body parts and brain tissue. Male DNA can exist inside cells in women bodies for decades. This effect was given the name microchimerism. The most studied cause of microchimerism is that originating from the male fetus into their pregnant mothers. However, women who have never been pregnant also had male DNA in their cells and it has been conducted that this was through sexual intercourse. Semen contains lymphocytes and other cells of the male which can pass into the bloodstream and continue to persist inside organs of women".

This study was done at the Fred Hutchinson cancer center in 2004, but can also be found looking up microchimerism on sites like NCBI, discovery, science mag and etc. One key part that stuck out to me was that this was done by taking blood samples which led me to Leviticus 17:11. The verse states, "For the life of the flesh is in the blood: and I have given it to you upon the alter to make an atonement for your souls: for it is the blood that makes an atonement for the soul". Many people will look at this verse and think it only meant for animal sacrifice but in verse 14 it clarifies it. Verse 14 states, "For it is the life of all flesh (humans too); the blood of it is the life thereof:" (Leviticus. 17:14). This study to me also confirmed how God created the woman out of the man in Genesis. And the rib, which the Lord God had taken from man, made he a woman, and brought her unto the man (Genesis. 2:22). When Genesis 2:22 explained the rib being removed from man to create the woman, we know that the rib consisted of Adam's DNA. So, every inch of the woman from head to toe was created out of the DNA of Adam, which explains how she was already his wife before they had intercourse. The process now is the DNA from semen covers every part of the woman's body. Judah told his son Onan to marry his brother's wife and raise kids unto his brother in Genesis 38:8. Verse 9 of Genesis 38 explained what the marrying process was based on Onan disobedience of not following through on his father command.

Organ	Presumed cell type	Maternal origin Mc	Fetal origin Mc
Brain	Neurons (murine)		X
Lymph node	Hematopoietic cells		X
Thyroid	Epithelial cells, thyrocytes		X
Blood	T cells, B cells, monocytes/ macrophages, NK cells, granulocytes	X	X
Blood	Lymphoid progenitor cells		X
Heart	Cardiac myocytes	X	X
Skin	Endothelial cells		X
Skin	Keratinocytes	X	
Spleen	Hematopoietic cells		X
Kidney	Renal tubular cells	X	
Pancreas	Islet beta cells	X	
Liver	Hepatocytes	X	X
Gallbladder	Epithelial cells		X
Intestine	Epithelial cells		X
Cervix	Epithelial cells		X

Modified from Nelson 2012

Figure 1: explains where the fetus cell can be detected within a woman.

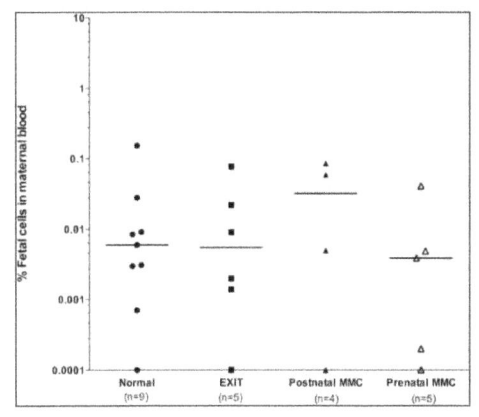

Figure 1

Maternal microchimerism. The percentage of maternal cells in cord blood was significantly different among groups (Kruskal Wallis for all groups, p=0.01. *= p<0.05 by pairwise comparison using Mann-Whitney; **= p<0.05 by Kruskal-Wallis ...

Figure 2: The blood difference between women regarding fetal cells.

Chapter 2
Effects of having multiple partners:
Men and Women

Now that I've explained how the cleaving process works in chapter 1, I can now explain the spiritual effects of your life from having multiple partners.

A reference regarding Sodom, "And all the people of Sodom and Gomorrah went there four times in the year, with their wives and children and all belonging to them, and they rejoiced there with timbrels and dances. And in the time of rejoicing they would all rise and lay hold of neighbor's wives, and some, the virgin daughters of their neighbors, and they enjoyed them, and each man saw his wife and daughter in the hands of his neighbor and did not say a word. And they did so from morning to night, and they afterward returned home each man to his house and each woman to her tent; so, they always did four times in the year" (Jasher. 18:13-15). For some of you that might check for references regarding this scripture, the book of Jasher is not in the regular pages of the bible. Instead the bible does verify the book in (Joshua. 10:13) & (2nd Samuel. 1:18). When I first read that passage, it immediately had me thinking of the club scene. In the club, just about everyone's there dressed to impress and "choosing" who they would like to go home with. In some cases, people have come into an event with one person and left with another.

I can remember in high school, running with a group of friends whose main goal was, to get with every girl they meet and keep status. The way we used to approach women, you would've thought we were car salesman. We had a strategic method, where we would avoid asking certain question to minimize the chances of rejection. Carnally thinking, you would say those were the good old days being young. Once you begin to understand spiritually what you are doing, you'll begin to see where a whole lot of mess in your life came from. In my next few paragraphs, I am going to use scenarios to explain the effects from both ends of having multiple partners. Before I do that, I want to explain in depths a few verses within Proverbs chapter 7.

The writer gave this description, "For at the window of my house I looked through my casement, and beheld among the simple ones, I discerned among the youths, A young man void of understanding, passing through the street near her corner; And he went the way to her house, In the twilight, in the evening, In the black and dark night: And behold, there met him a woman with the attire of a harlot, and subtil of heart" (Proverbs. 7:6-10). I believe it's possible when the writer wrote this, he was looking through a window in his house seeing the outside view. After the explanation regarding a house in the first chapter, I believe that the writer was explaining that he was witnessing the event. This was something unfolding before him and not a story handed down to him. I believe that description showed balance regarding a natural and spiritual level. The young man was simple, meaning he believed anything that someone would tell him. Biblical example, "The simple believeth every word: But the prudent look well to his going" (Proverbs. 14:15). He was also void of understanding just like many of us, especially not knowing the spiritual effects of having sexual intercourse.

    This story speaks out to me because I remember being that young man throughout life. I now understand how I have got into certain situation in my life. I wanted to write this book to make sure no more of our youths get caught up in situations like this. I believe once they really understand the spiritual effects, they would really think twice and hold themselves to a more higher value. This young man doesn't have any idea of what he is running into. You would think that the world is just a natural habitat and will end up walking into a spiritual trap. I have made that statement because I have been down this road before. Also, fathers teach your children their value and Impart in them spiritual things. When you not in your children lives, they will be in this world like sitting ducks, easy targets spiritually. This world will not spare or waste any time devouring them. The young man also met a woman with the attire of a harlot with a sneaky heart. This is not your ordinary woman, she is around to destroy lives physically and spiritually. She is not a harlot but dressed like one or should I say present herself as one, to capture your attention. She could be gorgeous, flashy in her fashion like she has a lot of money or getting her money from "tricking". She also can portray like she easily available (which would be the whole point of her trapping you). Very slick person that has a lot of game because she has a hidden agenda. I will speak further about her in my next chapter.

MEN: FROM HONORABLE TO DOGS

Paul's warning in this verse, "Flee fornication. Every sin that a man doeth is without the body; but he that committeth fornication sinneth against his own body" (1st Corinthians. 6:16). Therefore, it is very important to tell your young men to keep themselves holy until they find someone they want to be with for life. This segment is for that guy who considers himself an honorable person. Not experienced by worldly standards and kept himself pure. And it just so happens he stumbles across that one female who happens to be ratched.

This is what that's like spiritually, "For by means of a whorish woman a man is brought to a piece of bread: and the adulteress will hunt for the precious life" (Proverbs. 6:26). This woman, because she was able get men, most likely have got her prey by her cooking. That can be on a couple of levels, she can be very skillful in the kitchen, or she could have cursed his food to get him. I know some of you might ask, how can a ratched girl be an adulteress if she has never been married? On legal documents, she probably hasn't. Technically she has if she has had sex and the male cleave unto her. One example, "Whoso putteth away his wife, and marrieth another, committeth adultery: and whosoever marrieth her that is put away from her husband committeth adultery" (Luke. 16:18). Marriage during that time didn't consist of paperwork. The man dealt with her father and purchased her, for her token of virginity. The moment you cleave, the two flesh becomes one spiritually. And Judah said unto Onan, "Go in unto thy brother's wife, and marry her, and raise up seed unto thy brother" (Gen. 38:8). Understanding that, while in ignorance all the relationships and break ups that the woman went through, she was in adultery from the breakup of her very first relationship, to the most recent breakup. Back to the point, she looks good and dress good and usually don't have anything going for herself but a track record. Paul stated, "What? Know ye not that he which is joined to a harlot is one body? For two, saith he, shall be one flesh" (1st Corinthians 6:16).

    Dealing with her is like buying a house because of the paint job on the outside, only to find out everything wrong with it once you moved in. The heat doesn't work, pipes leaking, and you don't feel secure inside of it. The stress of it all can influence you. Also, it's like a child growing up in a broken home surrounded by drugs, alcohol, and sexual abuse. How can the child not be affected by their environment and possibly turn out the same way later down the road? Yes, if your environment is not comfortable to reside because it's haunted, not enough space, and from her past lovers it's like staying in a halfway house, these can have an impact on your life. It's amazing, a little while after I have put this scenario together to prove my point, God has showed me proof in the bible.

A good example of someone in the bible that was in a situation like this was King Solomon. Solomon started out great when he first became king and as time went on he ended up defiling himself. When Solomon became king of Israel, his father David told him to keep God first in everything you do, your walk, actions, lifestyle so God may continue his word regarding the house of David. Solomon did everything and exceeded his kingdom more than his father David. Solomon was at a place where he had peace on all sides of him and was able to build God's temple. Everything was well in Solomon's life until he decided to deal with numerous of women. The bible states, "But king Solomon loved many strange women, together with the daughter of Pharaoh, women of the Moabites, Ammonites, Edomites, Zidonians, and Hittites; of the nations concerning which the Lord said unto the children of Israel, Ye shall not go in to them, neither shall they come unto you: for surely, they will turn away your heart after their gods: Solomon clave unto these in love"

(1Kings. 11:1-2). The second verse of the passage I have just mentioned is very interesting. It explains the spiritual effect of having multiple partners. We know the pagan culture had all kinds of ungodly sex with each other far as orgies with men, women, children, and animals which made them along with their land defiled as explained in Leviticus the 18th chapter.

The obvious statement of explaining verse 2 is you shouldn't go into them and they shouldn't come into you. Those who worship false gods and you being joined to them, will cause you to turn your heart away from God. Looking at this verse really hit home for me (as it should for some of you), regarding turning your heart away. I know in our time we are not practicing pagan rituals like they did in biblical times or walking without grace like they did trying to keep the law; however, the effects remain the same years later. Let's say female XX is very materialistic, loves money, fashion, diamonds, cars, the spotlight which makes her covetous. Because of her coveting of the finer things also makes her an idolater. Male XY like wonderful things, but he really doesn't care for them. He doesn't think about these things often and it won't kill him if he doesn't have it. A few months passes by after they have cleaved together, he (XY) began to grow accustom to the flashy lifestyle after spending a lot of time with (XX). He also begins to view life the same way she does. What you have just witnessed is that XY heart began to turn to other gods which in this case was mammon and idolatry.

Another example let's say XY has attached to him a spirit of gluttony due to his love of food and XX has always watched her figure. After they have cleaved together, you'll notice XX begins to enjoy food a lot more. She begins to pick up weight, and her metabolism isn't as high as it used to be. As time continue to proceed, she began to become obese and can't figure out why. It's because the spirit of gluttony got in legally through cleaving with XY who already had it. In other cases, because of you or your partner had multiple partners in the past, the different personalities and spirits that was already attached, it could be possible that you may have had your heart turned to false gods. An example of the spiritual effect, "And he had seven hundred wives, princesses, and three hundred concubines: and his wives turned away his heart. For it came to pass, when Solomon was old, that his wives turned away his heart after other gods: and his heart was not perfect with the Lord his God, as was the heart of David his father" (1 Kings. 11:3-4). You mean to tell me just by laying with an unsaved or heathen woman can turn your heart away from God?

God's commandment to the Israelites, "Moreover, thou shalt not lie carnally with thy neighbor's wife to defile thyself with her" (Leviticus. 18:20). The verse is self-explanatory, laying around just to soil your royal oats (from coming to America lol). This is for the players in the game, getting in where they fit in. While you are keeping status, you are defiling yourself losing value. I wish I would have known these things then. These guys spiritually, are like unstable tenants that move several times throughout the year. Not only they bring in too much mess, but they leave behind mess as well. James wrote, "A double minded man is unstable in all his ways" (James. 1:8). I know, because I used to be like this. I was either driven by my own understanding or by my lust and my life had reflected it. An old proverb stated, "He that loveth pleasure shall be a poor man: he that loveth wine and oil shall not be rich" (Proverbs. 21:17). Because of what guys do usually for pleasure, they don't know that they're releasing their soul (along with any other spirits) upon many women, which usually wreck their lives out of control. Therefore, you will see them watching every female moving or acting like a dog in heat. They have scattered themselves everywhere and other women usually reminds them where their soul has gone or where lust want to take them.

    Most guys spiritually don't recover or renounce from the ties he connected with while being single. What's worse than that, is married guys playing the game. "But whoso committed adultery with a woman lacketh understanding: he that doeth it destroyed his own soul" (Proverbs. 6:32). I believe when the bible stated "lacketh understanding", I believe it was talking about the spiritual effect of sex. The woman who made a covenant to you were to get all of you, but since you are scattering yourself, your wife is only left with a piece. Here an example, say XY wife don't understand where he's coming from at times, but his former girlfriend knows and is easy to talk to about it. I believe that happens because, while he was dealing with his former girlfriend she was able to receive that part of him.

It's important to renounce from those ties and break that covenant especially after you get married or on a new walk with Christ. The effect of the player married result is, "A wound and dishonor shall he get; and his reproach shall not be wiped away. For jealousy is the rage of a man: Therefore, he will not spare in the day of vengeance" (Proverbs. 6:33-34). There are many ways to receive a wound spiritually by this action. You can receive a broken heart, or a disease just to name a couple. Also, it can just so happen you end up with someone who couldn't wait to spill the beans. It's possible even the bible states it, "The words of a talebearer are as wounds, and they go down into the innermost parts of the belly" (Proverbs. 26:22). Second precept, "A talebearer revealeth secrets: (Proverbs. 11:13a). Now looking at that second precept, it does makes sense. You are being unfaithful and messing with someone else who is most likely unfaithful, what else would you expect. Not only that, you must also deal with a jealous and perhaps crazy husband or boyfriend. That's a new enemy that you must deal with, which is very unnecessary. Because jealousy is the rage of a man, that is like giving him legal right to be upset at you because you violated him. The bible also states, "So, he that goeth into his neighbor's wife; whosoever toucheth her shall not be innocent" (Proverbs. 6:29).

While you are married, you will go to great lengths to cover your tracks, just like David in 2nd Samuel chapter 11. David seen Uriah wife washing up, he fetched for her and ended up laying with her. David went through great lengths to cover his tracks once he found out that Uriah's wife was pregnant. He tried to have Uriah sleep with her by getting him drunk enough to do so. Once he found out that didn't work, he eventually had him killed in war. David spot was blown up by Nathan the prophet when his secret sin was revealed. God ended up striking the baby that was conceived from adultery and the baby ended up dying.

WOMEN: FROM VIRTUOUS TO HARLOTS

Jacob's sons replied, "And they said, should he deal with our sister as with a harlot?" (Genesis. 34:31). Earlier in that chapter Shechem seen Jacob's daughter Dinah and when he saw her, took, lay and defiled her. The steps he took to lay with Dinah is something that would have been done to harlots. It's funny how songs today target our women and young ladies to wreck their lives. With catchphrases like "bad guys are no good, but good guys are no fun" and "why do good girls like bad guys". In a real situation, a good girl having a bad guy spiritually, is like the movie the Beverly hillbillies. The movie is about a bunch of raggedy hillbillies that inherits a beautiful mansion. The guy who inherits the mansion moves in with his family, dirty laundry, animals, and piles of junk. Throughout the movie, you began to see the house deteriorate and diminish in value. That's the same spiritually, with someone that's a virtuous woman and letting some dog of a guy reside in your house. You can be affected by his mess, and you must repent and renounce that day it happened, to shake his soul off you. "Give not that which is holy unto dogs, neither cast your pearls before swine, lest they trample them under their feet, and turn again and rend you" (Matthew. 7:6). Give away nothing that is very valuable to something or someone that is unclean, because it will bite you in the end. Holy in this case would be your house, your innocence and virtue. Dogs on the other hand are humans with that animal spirit. During biblical time, they were Baal's priest that practiced all types of pagan sex with the people that came into their temple to worship.

For women, it's different for them to have multiple partners, because they are the receivers. Because they're able to attract multiple personalities along with spirits from different guys, they can easily become schizophrenic. In Proverbs, it states "For her house inclineth unto death, and her path unto the dead" (Proverbs. 2:18). It's funny how you can easily end up in a life or death situation messing with certain women. Her path or track record usually consist of guys who are spiritually dead. They don't know God or have rejected God and blinded by society's way of life. Women, it's like having tenants instead of a buyer residing at your residence, they're only around temporary. The least might be broken, and you'll be left to repair all the wears and tears. Some women really treat their bodies like slum landlords. Instead of repairing the wears and tears, they figure they can cover it up and move in the next tenant, and keep the money rolling. A lot of time, some women have multiple partners chasing after money. They'll make the mistake of choosing a "baller" over a hardworking man for financial stability. Proverbs declared, "Wealth gotten by vanity shall be diminished: but he that gathereth by labor shall increase" (Proverbs. 13:11). Because of this choice of a guy, they usually end up with bad memories and housing multiple souls. That usually ends up being more damage done to your house and the cost of fixing can begin to become steep.

SOUL TIES STUDY CONTINUED

Microchimerism study shows that in every 100,000 female cells there are 0 (that's being the least) to 20.7% (that's 20,700) of male cells (that's near one fifth). The higher percentage rate that can be detected could relate to the multiple partners that the female had. What also is another shocking study, women having multiple children by multiple partners die faster than women who haven't had multiple partners. This came paraphrased studying health consequences of microchimerism at pubmed.gov and redpill.com.

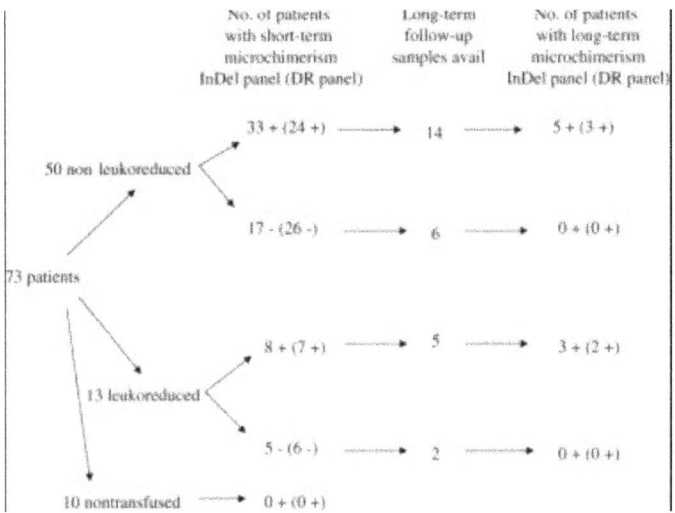

Figure 3: Shows the long-term and short-terms effects of microchimerism.

Chapter 3
Beauty is vain:

Because it can have it cons

Regarding a virtuous woman, a verse also stated, "Favour is deceitful, and beauty is vain: but a woman that feareth the Lord, she shall be praised" (Proverbs. 31:30). To all women, there's nothing wrong with being beautiful, it shows to have many benefits. History throughout society shows that many opportunities comes with having a beautiful face and or a body. Because of that, some women had all expense paid trips, their bills covered monthly, shopping sprees, spots on TV shows and or movies, possibly a wedding ring and a wedding. Nothing is wrong with having wonderful things and living comfortably. If that's all what you are living for, you are heading for destruction very fast. The writer quoted in Proverbs, "Wilt thou set thine eyes upon that which is not? For riches certainly make themselves wings; they fly as an eagle towards heaven" (Proverbs. 23:5). The more you chase after it, the more the goal will seem out of reach. Although you are living stable, you'll always want more and is never satisfied. When you have that kind of mentality ladies, Satan is going to always use a guy with his money to torture you. No, I don't mean like the movie "hostel"-type torture (although that can possibly happen).

The fact he has money and you're gold-digging or "thirsty", he can use it as a leverage to control you. He can mistreat you using it, dangle it in your face while giving you little. He can do what he wants because he knows that you will put up with it. Why would some women rather choose materialistic values over their dignity (true value)? In this chapter, I'm going to touch on the spiritual marine kingdom, that uses the natural beauty for bait. Also, touching on the entrapment for men and women and becoming a victim because of your beauty.

    This is where your discernment should come in, because not everyone is who they say they are. Marine spirits, like mermaids and mermen comes in the form of humans. Their main purpose is to get involved with you just to wreck your life. Some marine spirits manifest in human form, while others can inhabit the human body. They also can initiate people into their kingdom through outlets like entertainment, internet, foods etc... Marine spirits come from the spiritual marine kingdom. Just like how the physical aquatic life is in the water, they have a spiritual realm as well. It is rooted in African and Haitian witchcraft, where they worshipped who they call Mami Wata in exchange for wealth. This kingdom uses wealth as an enticement to lure people in and to spiritually bound them. Mainly, this kingdom produces the spirits behind sexual perversion, lust, sexual revealing clothing, make up, eyeliner and lipstick (all for seduction). Some of your dreams you may have about water, fishes, marriage in your dream to a husband or wife, and even sex in your dream, is them waging an attack against you. Have you noticed when you have sex in your dream it just happens, nothing leads up to it, like it starts out of nowhere? As a result of sex or marriage in the dream can be the cause of why some people can't or won't get married. If they were to get married, it won't last long, and some end up having multiple marriages. The reason being is because they became one with a spirit spouse through their dream and that spirit runs everyone away from them.

The marine kingdom is in the bible and I'll give a few examples from my studies. I'm doing so because at first, I wasn't sure of this kingdom when I have heard about it. Here's an example of how spirits operate, "So the devils besought him saying, if thou cast us out, suffer us to go into the herd of swine" (Matthew. 8:31). I wanted to know why the devils asked Jesus to go into the swine? In Leviticus, it states, "And the swine, though he divides the hoof, and he be clovenfooted, yet he cheweth not the cud; he is unclean to you" (Leviticus. 11:7). Basically, the devils attach themselves to anything that is unclean. Uncleanness is any sins, bitterness, or resentment that you didn't seek God for forgiveness of or anything you haven't forgave anyone about. Jesus responded, "And he said unto them, Go. And when they were come out, they went into the herd of swine: and behold, the whole herd of swine ran violently down a steep place into the sea, and perished in the waters" (Matthew. 8:32). These spirts were given a license to possess or even attach themselves to anything that is unclean. The swine running down a steep place represents that person's life going on a destructive downward spiral, which is the effect of that kingdom. Also, the swine physically dies but the devils didn't. They must find a new body to torment and bring to hell while they have the time.

    Another example of the marine kingdom, "Speak, and say, thus saith the Lord God; Behold, I am against thee, Pharaoh king of Egypt, the great dragon that lieth in the midst of his rivers, which hath said, my river is mine own, and I have made for myself" (Ezekiel. 29:3). We all know who the great dragon was, but notice where he was operating from at that time. When Egypt was establishing power and later became a global domination they were under the guidance from Joseph. Then we read in the bible, "Now there arose up a new king over Egypt, which knew not Joseph" (Exodus. 1:8). We knew Joseph was a man of God that followed God in all his ways. The people who Joseph was governing over would've followed God also. This king that didn't know Joseph, also didn't know God the Father as well. He was operating under a different source of spiritual guidance. Back to shedding the light on the dragon. God stated, "But I will put hooks in thy jaws, and I will cause the fish of thy rivers to stick unto thy scales, and I will bring thee up out of the midst of thy rivers, and all the fish of thy rivers shall stick unto thy scales" (Ezekiel. 29:4). God's kingdom trumps all kingdoms, "And God made two great lights; the greater light to rule the day and the lesser light to rule the light: he made the stars also" (Genesis. 1:16). God have defeated the source of power from the river. Not only that, once the dragon was removed all his minions was also dealt with. This wasn't a physical dragon in the river and it wasn't physical fishes that stuck to his scales. Remember this was a prophecy concerning the pharaoh in Exodus.

In pharaoh's global domination, this was like a one world government on a smaller scale. Who was the great dragon in the prophecy? Biblical answer, "And the great dragon was cast out, that old serpent, called the devil, and Satan, which deceiveth the whole world: he was cast out into the earth, and his angels were cast out with him" (Revelation. 12:9). Satan was operating his one world government from the waters. Satan being defeated, "Thus saith the Lord, in this thou shalt know that I am the Lord: behold, I will smite with the rod that is in mine hand upon the waters which are in the river, and they shall be turned into blood. And the fish that is in the river shall die, and the river shall stink; and the Egyptains shall lothe to drink of the water of the river. And the Lord spake unto Moses, say unto Aaron, take thy rod, and stretch out thine hand upon the waters of Egypt, upon their streams, upon all their rivers, and upon their ponds, and upon all their pools of water, that they may become blood; and that there may be blood throughout all the land of Egypt, both in vessels of wood, and in vessels of stone" (Exodus. 7:17-19).

The natural fish that was in the water was cursed because the dragon was the source of the reproduction of the water. Every time the people of that land ate the fish and drink of the water they were getting initiated into that spiritual kingdom, which also assisted in the bondage of the people. Before the rod was used to destroy everything, the river, wood, and stone was being worshipped. Satan along with other demons were receiving the praise. Because of that, the blood being physically revealed in the waters shows that the demonic powers were being smitten and was rendered powerless. I would go further into details regarding this story, but that will be during another subject, which isn't about sex.

One last verse showing there is a marine kingdom. "And I saw another angel ascending from the east, having the seal of the living God: and he cried with a loud voice to the four angels, to whom it was given to hurt the earth and the sea, saying, hurt not the earth, neither the sea, not the trees, til we have sealed the servants of our God in their foreheads" (Revelation 7:2-3). Those are a few examples of verses showing there's a spiritual marine kingdom. There are mermaid and mermen coming into the earth posing as human like Ariel in the little mermaid. As an assignment, I encourage every teen and adult to watch that movie with discernment and see how the spiritual marine kingdom operates. Here's another example of how they work, "For of this sort are they which creep into houses, and lead captive silly women laden with sins, led away with divers' lusts" (2 Timothy 3:6). This particular verse is describing worldly thinking women with no spiritual understanding who usually get lead away captive. With your own lust ladies, you can be led away from God.

Drawn to wanting the finer things until you are at the point of idolizing material things. This is how women usually end up with a marine spirit in them. All it would take is to get involved with a guy, who just so happens to have everything you lust after. On the flip side, this is for the fellas, "For her house inclineth unto death, and her path unto the dead. None that go unto her return again, neither they take hold the paths of life" (Proverbs. 2:18-19). With this kind of a woman, you usually would deal with a lot of unnecessary drama. Not only that, possibly end up in a life or death situation. Her track record consists of former lovers who are spiritually dead. These people consist of murderers, drug dealers (sorcerers), oath takers (freemasons and frat members), usually bad people that have a lot of material wealth. These particular guys are stuck in their worldly way of thinking and living with no desire of wanting to live righteously. Those are outcome of being involved with them.

SPIRITUAL ENTRAPMENT FOR BOTH MEN AND WOMEN

Remember in chapter 2 when I stated I was going to explain the spirit of the women in Proverbs 7 starting at verse 11. This woman didn't come from the water, but has the marine spirit residing in her. Chapter 7 in Proverbs breaks down how she operates. Pertaining to this spirit, "She is loud and stubborn; her feet abide not in her house:

The Spiritual Effects of Sex

Now is she without, now in the streets, and lieth in wait at every corner" (Proverbs. 7:11-12). She's usually a "ratched chickenhead" who idolized and worship herself, "stubbornness is as iniquity and idolatry" (1 Samuel. 15:23b). She also came from a good family, but she's the only one that's into the wicked way of living. Don't usually have anything and isn't about nothing. If she were to have anything, she will only obtain it momentarily. Once you get with her everything around her will began to fall apart. Repo-man coming for the vehicle and the landlord is ready to throw her on the streets. In biblical times these women were walking the stroll then, just as they do now. Also, she at these clubs, bars, and events where street people go. I know that one person can't physically be at every corner, but that same spirit she has is everywhere the nightlife is.

Operation of this spirit continues, "So she caught him, and kissed him, and with an impudent face said unto him, I have peace offerings with me; this day have I payed my vows. Therefore, I came to meet thee, diligently to seek thy face and I have found thee: (Proverbs. 7:13-15). She chased after him and came on to him sexually, he didn't even have to choose her. The same way the serpent came in a submissive position towards the woman. The spirit in her took control of the situation, to run her game on her prey. She came off like she "balling" or the ideal independent chick. She insists that she can even treat you and she just out celebrating. She might have even stated that she had to approach you and not miss this opportunity to be with you. She was looking for your type, because something about you may stick out from every other guy. It could be your vulnerability, gullible or you are a fresh new prey. The more she talks, the more you'll notice that she has been watching you the whole time. She has done her homework, and this was not something that was done off instinct.

    Her tactic isn't finished, "I have deckt my bed with coverings of tapestry, with carved works, with fine linen of Egypt. I have perfumed my bed with myrrh, aloes, and cinnamon. Come, let us take our fill of love until the morning: let us solace ourselves with loves" (Proverbs. 7:16-18). She portrays herself to be bigger than what she is. Keep in mind about the statement earlier about her when it stated "she was without". She claims to only get the best, but she only telling you that, so you can get it for her. When she gets things, she can't afford to hold on to it because she buys things way out of her budget. Naturally, she wants to get up with you for that one-night stand and see how far things can go between you guys. Spiritually, she really wants to get up with you, to have you in her house (soul tie). Once you reside there she'll begin draining and wrecking your life. Last statement concerning the operation, "For the Goodman is not at home, he is gone a long journey: He hath taken a bag of money with him and will come home at the day appointed. With her much fair speech she caused him to yield, with the flattering of her lips she forced him" (Proverbs. 7:19-21). This woman doesn't fear God nor have him in her heart. Also, the same verse tells us she had a past relationship and is now single. The guy either left her, cheating while he gone, or maybe he even locked up. Everything she has going on, ties into her game that she runs on her victims. The guy will usually think, he has hit the jackpot and got himself a winner. He might even think the possibilities are endless with them as a couple. That was a blueprint how this spirit operates in women trapping men. There are many other ways, just to keep alert.

      Guys, when things sound too good to be true it usually is. As instructed in Proverbs, "To keep thee from the evil woman, from the flattery tongue of a strange woman. Lust not after her beauty in thine heart; neither let her take thee with her eyelids" (Proverbs. 6:25). Wanting to be with her is all you are thinking about and her eyes she uses to seduce you. Also, "Let not thine heart decline to her ways, go not astray in her paths" (Proverbs. 7:25). Be your own man, don't do what she does. Basically, in a nutshell stop chasing her validation. If she only dated unrighteous people who have a lot of money, don't desire to be like them, to impress her or even keep her. She wants to be the reason of you not getting close with God, falling out with God or your life going in a downward spiral. Women please pay attention, "And whereas thou sawest iron mixt with miry clay, they shall mingle themselves with the seed of men: but they shall not cleave one to another, even as iron is not mixed with clay" (Daniel. 2:43). This verse explains, not only can people be possessed, but these spirits can even have sex with people (incubus and succubus). They shall not have a union like how a real marriage is, because iron don't mix with clay. I believe this verse is specific for the women, (especially the ones) who think they can be successful by being a groupie. Newsflash, if you think you can get your favorite male celebrity hooked with your pocketbook (old school term), it won't happen. It won't happen, because he has another spirit in him that won't cleave to you through sex. That same spirit (along with the individual) will fulfil its lust.

God's warning while you are living in this world, "Regard not them that have familiar spirits, neither seek after wizards, to be defiled by them" (Leviticus. 19:3). Based on John Todd's testimony, who was big in the record business, stated, "after the 70's an artist must be an initiated witch in order to have a recording contract". Side note, males are not called witches but wizards and being defiled by someone is usually sexual. Remember Jacob's daughter explained earlier in chapter 2? I don't know the exact words of a recording contract, but it would basically state (if the signature is signed in blood), that the body and soul of the individual is in the control of a demonic spirit for entertainment purposes (which is to influence the masses (people)). So, my next question would be (after now knowing), is the money or living your dreams physically, really worth it spiritually?

BECOMING A VICTIM BECAUSE OF BEAUTY

Fellas pay attention, "For she cast down many wounded: yea, many strong men have been slain by her" (Proverbs. 7:26). The first part (cast down many wounded) speaks about vulnerable guys, who cannot handle being rejected by women. Although they can't handle rejection, they desperately seek after someone and will take just about anyone. They have what is called a scarcity mindset. That's the opposite of what Jesus taught because he wanted you to live life more abundantly. They'll run across her, sleep with her and she'll begin draining them out physically, spiritually, or even both. If the guy was financially stable, he will pick up her problems as well as his own and begin struggling. He will continue to struggle until he no longer has anything.

I had a neighbor once, he was an older gentleman who had retired and was living comfortably. He didn't have no spouse living with him, just his grandson. His grandson was used to being spoiled by him. When the grandson got older he wanted to make fast money. He was into gambling and spending his winnings, then his thirst grew. One night he committed a crime (that's all I'm telling) and have been identified by the victim. Because of that he ended up having to serve a prison sentence. While the grandson was away on his state sponsored vacation the grandfather became very lonely. He would talk with my mom whenever she was available and me sometimes before I have moved from my mother's house. Fast forward to a few years, I was visiting my mother's house one day and I have seen my neighbor outside of his home.

He was standing outside with a few of his family members, very distraught. It looked like he woke up from under a spell. His family members were telling him that he must get off the property and was making plans for his living arrangements. While doing that, they were also asking him, how did you let this happen? Where is your money? Etc. When I was approaching them I thought, it was like a little reunion, so I introduced myself. They spoke back, but their facial expression meant business. So, I went into my mom's house and asked what was going on? She and my God sister explained, due to the loneliness of not having his grandson around, he started dating this woman. This woman was known to have a drug problem and may have been a street walker (an official harlot). When he started dating her, he was splurging on her often. While he was doing that, she must've got access to his money and was spending it like it was hers. She was sneaking the evidence along with some of his things out the back door. When it came time to pay the mortgage or taxes he didn't have it. He eventually had to be removed from the property and make living arrangements.

The second part of the verse of Proverbs 7:26 (many strong men are slain by her). Explains the situation of someone being grounded in the word or at least knows what the bible says. "A wise man is strong; yea, a man of knowledge increaseth strength" (Proverbs. 24:5). Somehow, they'll still manage to get themselves caught up dealing with these marine spirits. If they don't know the word, they at least are usually up on game coming from the world. Some situations, the guy is usually being grounded in both on game and in the word. They usually are in a far worse situation because their life is at stake. That marine spirit assignment is to set them up to get killed before they can repent.

    King David's son Absalom had a very gorgeous sister named Tamar. David's other son Ammon, was in love with her. The bible states, "And Ammon was so vexed, that he fell sick for his sister Tamar; for she was a virgin; and Ammon thought it hard for him to do anything with her" (2 Samuel. 13:2). Ammon lusted after her so bad that he made himself literally sick over her. He begins to plot how he was going to make his lust a reality. Ammon had a friend who also was his cousin named Jonadab, who wanted to know what was wrong with him. Ammon told his cousin how he was in love with his brother's sister Tamar. Jonadab is a subtil kind of guy (a schemer, manipulator), has come up with a game plan for him, Ammon ended up following through with it. When it was time for Ammon to make his move, he has Tamar cooking for him and told everyone else to leave. When Tamar was done cooking for him and was bringing his food to him, he asked her to lay (sleep) with him. She told him no and tried to talk him out of it, "like you are out of your mind" (emphasis added) and you will bring shame unto the family. After all of that, "Howbeit he would not hearken unto her voice: but, being stronger than she, forced her, and lay with her. Then Ammon hated her exceedingly; so, that the hatred wherewith he hated her was greater than the love wherewith he loved her. And Ammon said unto her arise, be gone" (2 Samuel. 13:14-15). The spirit of lust, which is rooted in covetousness (Romans. 7:7) controlled Ammon so bad where he raped his brother's sister to fulfill it. After the lustful spirit gets what it wants, it's never completely satisfied. It will continue to the next person or next level of sexual desire. This story is an example where I mentioned the definition of cleaving as meaning to split apart during sexual intercourse.

Tamar stated, "And she said unto him, there is no cause: this evil in sending me away is greater than the other that thou didst unto me. But he would not hearken unto her. Then he called his servant that ministered unto him, and said, put now this woman out from me, and bolt the door after her" (2 Samuel. 13:16-17). Maybe not the incest part, but ladies have you been in a situation where a guy drops you off or had one of his boys to drop you off after having sex with you? You have fulfilled the lustful spirit that was the driving force behind him. I know because I been there before dropping off someone for myself, friends, and family members. I thank the Lord from where he brought me from and able to share my experience along with knowledge, wisdom, and understanding. Encouraging our younger generation to do things God's way and shaping my generation and the generations prior before it's too late.

STUDIES REGARDING BEAUTY PRODUCTS AND ENTRAPMENTS

I was reading an article regarding the queen of the coast and her strategic plan of wreaking havoc upon the church (and the earth). She had minions under her to carry out her order, and if they failed they consider themselves dead. One of the thing she said concerning people she quotes, "walking naked without any cloth". This is her spiritual vision referring to people who haven't accepted the Lord in their lives, they can easily be used to assist them in their wickedness. She also stated, "They are the one we will use for celebration, after our victory, we will eat their flesh and drink their blood by December, and use the remaining blood to prepare more lipsticks, jewelries and cosmetics for the foolish woman among them".

There are a lot of things that was brought up in that statement I want to address. Eating the flesh and drinking the blood, I wanted to know if they're doing this physically or spiritually, and what the bible says about it. Another thing I wanted to know is blood an active ingredient in lipstick and other cosmetic? Also, what the bible states concerning foolish women. Another statement that the queen of the coast made in this article was concerning powder, not sure if it was special powder or powder used for makeup. She stated, "I have given you enough power and cosmetic to make even women lust after you. I've given you enough trainings, those powder I've given you are very powerful, use it and souls who refuse to run into the secret place of the Lord and live under his shadow, will lust after you. This powder is the ashes of those who fail the task I gave to them. If you fail yours too, you will be grind into ashes". After reading that I wanted to know if some powder were really made of ashes because that statement has some serious claims.

    While investigating I have found some strange things that are in cosmetics. Whale poop or vomit has been used for some expensive perfumes. Lipsticks contains beetles that has been crushed up. These beetles eat red cactus berries. When the beetles get crushed red dye is produced. Fish scales are found in nail polish and mascara. Roadkill is found in lipstick, eye shadow and soap. Bull semen can be found in some hair products, and dynamite in some deodorant and exfoliants. Snail ooze and infant foreskins can be found in moisturizers. Wool wax from a sheep is in shaving cream; and shark liver oil in lip balm, sunscreen and more. The Food and Drug Administration recently told cosmetics makers to stop using the brains and spinal cord tissue from older cows in products like lipstick and hair spray to try to prevent the spread of mad cow disease to humans. The same ingredient is considered ok if the cow was 30 months old or younger.

    The infant foreskin was interesting because it's bloody process concerning circumcision. In Exodus, it states, "Then Zipporah took a sharp stone, and cut off the foreskin of her son, and cast it at her feet, and said, surely a bloody husband art thou to me. So, he let him go: then she said, a bloody husband thou art, because of the circumcision" (Exodus. 4:25-26). Concerning the foolish woman, "A foolish woman is clamorous: she is simple, and knoweth nothing" (Proverbs. 9:13). This the type of women that will follow any trend and tends to jump into thing headfirst, not knowing it might cost her later in life.

Chapter 4
Masturbation:

Powers that are within an image

I can remember when I first started at my former job working with mentally disabled individuals who have committed sex crimes. They were put on restrictions from normal activities as a part of their treatment. I was young when I first started and was shocked because the individuals' I was monitoring were way older than me (except for a few who was around my age). I wanted to know the reason for the restrictions for these adults. It wasn't until I have gone to one of their group session while I was in training. Their restrictions such as what they can watch on TV, where they can go far as in the community, along with other things were in detail. I have asked a psychologist can he explain the reason for the restrictions that they have for their treatment. What he explained always stuck in my head and I never knew why (besides doing my job of course), until I have decided to write this book.

I'm paraphrasing the actual statement, due to their sexual attraction which led them to committing their sexual crimes, certain programs on TV and certain events in the community they weren't allowed to engage in. The reason being because it can trigger their old habits and add fuel to their desires. Now since growing in the Lord I know what that means spiritually. Psychology always try to explain away spiritual things or spirits, naturally. To the individuals that were trying their treatment program, those things would be a stumbling block to them and perhaps their deliverance. The individuals that wasn't complying with their treatment, what they would do is find a way to have access to what they were restricted from. They know they can't have it for long, so they will take a photographic memory of it. After storing that memory in their head, they would go into their room to masturbate. This was adding fuel to their lustful desire they have burning inside them. While spiraling in that direction this can increase their chance of offending again to fulfill their lustful spirit.

Masturbation would seem harmless naturally because you not hurting anyone while you are releasing tension. Spiritually you are only setting yourself up for gateways opening and bondage. You are fulfilling that lustful spirit inside of you which will never be satisfied. You'll be on a journey to wanting to fulfill more fantasies or fetishes and receive more spirits. There are more than what you normally think when it comes to masturbation. We all know that sex is a form of worship, there's a correct way which glorifies God and other ways (which are pagan) that glorifies different deities' aka demons. What are you worshipping when you are masturbating? Believe it or not it's a graven image. God commanded, "Thou shalt not make unto thee any graven image, or any likeness of anything that is in heaven above, or that is in the earth beneath, or that is in the waters under the earth: (Exodus. 20:4).

    The first part of the verse I asked myself how would someone make unto themselves a graven image? Normally, I have thought of drawing, painting, and sculpturing until I looked up the definition. Graven image as a noun is an object (such as a statue) that is worshipped as a god or in place of a god, carved usually from wood and stone. That's what I have expected far as definition. Thing became interesting when I have looked both words separately. When I looked up graven, it took me to grave as a transitive verb; which is normally dig, carve with a chisel or engrave letters. The last meaning of the verb stunned me, it means to impress or fix (as a thought) deeply. When I have seen that I was done, I wasn't going to look up the definition of the word image, but I did just to confirm my point. Image is a picture that is produced by a camera, artist, mirror, etc, the mental picture: the thought of how something looks or might look: the idea that people have about someone or something. In other words, graven image is deeply thinking of something where you can almost visualize it. The actual image that was created (whether by painting, or carving) is a manifestation of what was in someone head. That image in their mind can become so bad where they can make a physical appearance of it. Masturbating while thinking deeply of an image (or watching it on TV) can cause you to be joined to a spirit that behind the image.

It all starts in the mind before it becomes a visual image whatever it may be. Paul wrote, "For the weapons of our warfare are not carnal, but mighty through God to the pulling down of strongholds; casting down imaginations, and every high thing that exalteth itself against the knowledge of God, and bringing into captivity every thought to the obedience of Christ;" (1 Corinthians. 10:4-5). By looking at these verses, it lets me know that the spiritual attack that we deal with usually manifest itself naturally. That's done to cause us to react naturally in hoping that will resolve the issue. Imagination is rooted from image which starts in the mind. Part of our spiritual weapons that we used is thinking wisely. Every thought that run across your mind good or bad you would have to give it a background check and see if it lines up with God's word. The primal part of the spiritual battle starts in the mind first before it can cause you to go astray. The bible states it, "Or else how can enter into a strong man's house, and spoil his goods, except he first bind the strong man? And then he will spoil his house" (Matthew. 12:29). Explaining further this verse, it starts off with the enemy sowing thoughts in your head contrary to God's word. It can start off with people that have a bad influence and what your attention (evil communications corrupt good manners). By you not bringing those thoughts into captivity and also listening to them, those spirits are binding the strong man. They start from the outside and work their way in with Satan devices or people who have them. Don't believe that's binding the strongman?

Proverbs states, "A wise man is strong; yea, a man of knowledge increaseth strength" (Proverbs. 24:5). If they can corrupt your thinking to how they want you to think, it won't be long before you act on it. Once you're down that road you'll begin to think there's nothing wrong with it.

Another effect that comes from masturbation that no males usually think about, (because they are thinking of themselves when they do it) is slaughtering the innocent. Never thought of that? Me neither at one point, but it is just as bad as abortion. The punishment of that sin was death, thank God for his grace for not understanding spiritually. There is one character in the bible wasn't as lucky. Proving my point, "And Judas begat Phares and Zara of Thamar; And Phares begat Esrom; and Esrom begat Aram;" (Matthew. 1:3). I wanted to point out this specific part of the lineage along with other scriptures before I bring my conclusion.

In Genesis, it states, "And Judah took a wife for Er his firstborn, whose name was Tamar. And Er, Judah firstborn was wicked in the sight of the Lord; and the Lord slew him. And Judah said unto Onan, go in unto thy brother's wife, and marry her, and raise up seed to thy brother. And Onan knew that the seed should not be his; and it came to pass, when he went in unto his brother's wife, that he spilled it on the ground, lest that he should give seed to his brother. And the thing which he did displeased the Lord: wherefore he slew him also" (Genesis. 38:6-10). Judah said to Onan, go in unto thy brother's wife, and marry her, this part of that verse proved my point regarding the earlier chapters. The moment the cleaving happens you are considered married and having multiple partners would consider you to be an adulterous. I wanted to know how Onan was going to raise seed for his brother Er, seeing that they were their own individual? My guess for it being a possibility is because both individuals have the same parents. Taking it a step further the 23 chromosomes that comes from Judah and the other 23 chromosomes that comes from Judah's wife, who is the daughter of Shuah. Since the lineage goes through the father according to the bible, it would be more of Judah and Shuah DNA. Shuah daughter, Judah's wife would be an incubator (the soil or earth that develops the seed). Er, Onan, and Shelah would have the same genetic marker due to their parents far as the rolls of each chromosomes plays.

Back to the story, after the first two of Judah's son died, Tamar (who was originally the firstborn sons' wife) was to remain a widow at her father's house until the youngest son Shelah became groan, and she were to marry him. As time pass, Shelah became groan and she was not given to be his wife. This is the same thing spiritually that will happen to you when false prophecies have been spoken in your life. You'll sit around wasting your time and waiting for something that was told to you by someone lying to you about your future. I'm pretty sure when she realized that it wasn't going to happen she became upset. Tamar received info on where her father

The Spiritual Effects of Sex

and law was going to be. So, she removed her widow's garment to put on a harlot's garment (which covered her face), to deceive Judah because she felt played by him. Around this same time, Judah's wife had died already so when him and Tamar met, they met as "Jon" and "harlot". They exchanged transaction a staff, signet and bracelet for a good time. So, when Judah was back in town and heard that Tamar was pregnant, he was upset and wanted to charge her. Tamar response was everything she received from the transaction, "whoever these belong to, that's who I'm pregnant by". When Judah seen, them, he felt guilty because he didn't hold up his end of the bargain of giving her to his youngest son.

Genesis states, "And it came to pass, when she travailed, that the one put out his hand: and the midwife took and bound upon his hand a scarlet thread, saying, this came out first. And it came to pass, as he drew back his hand, that behold, his brother came out: and she said, how hast thou broken forth? This breach be upon thee: therefore, his name was called Pharez. And afterward came out his brother, that had the scarlet thread upon his hand: and his name was called Zarah" (Genesis. 38:28-30). This story shows how the Lineage started through Judah and Tamar, who was originally his sons' wife. Had both of his sons or at least one of them had been obedient instead of wicked, Pharez and Zarah were supposed to be Judah's grandsons instead of his sons. If God didn't make a way for Judah and Tamar to hook up, which eventually had the Messiah Jesus Christ come through that lineage. What

Onan did by spilling his seed out of selfishness was like an assassination attempt, stopping Jesus from coming through Judah's Lineage to save the world from their sins.

STUDIES REGARDING MASTURBATION

Some men claimed when they gave up masturbation they gained higher energy levels, better skin, and enhancement within their self-confidence. On the contrary, there have been some studies that has been in favor of masturbation. Their report stated, "those who masturbated report to have better physical and psychological health compared to those who don't masturbate". Also, they claimed it's linked to higher self-esteem among women, while it lowers the likelihood of men developing prostate cancer. In men, it increases in cells which helps fights off infection, while in women it may prevent certain cervical infections. The women cervix opens up during sexual arousal, allowing bacteria to be flushed out. The list goes on and on stating, "In females they have happier marriages and more satisfying sex then the ones that don't masturbate". After everything I have just mentioned regarding what they called benefits, when you examine it, it only pleases the flesh.

Charles Leadbeater, who was a part of the Theosophical Society in the early 1900's taught a sexual technique to an inner circle of initiates who claimed that, "the energy aroused in masturbation can be used as a form of occult power, a great release of energy which can first, elevate the consciousness of the individual to a state of ecstasy, and second, direct a great rush of psychic force towards the logos for his use in occult work".

Chapter 5
Homosexuality:

Going against the Godly order

    This topic has been controversial over the years, to the point it has brought us to our current state. It shows us as humans our current state with God, we are wrestling with him. In Paul's Letter to Ephesus , "For we wrestle not against flesh and blood, but against principalities, against powers, against the rulers of the darkness of this world, against spiritual wickedness in high places" (Ephesians. 6:12). The wrestle isn't physical but spiritual. Believers in Christ, wrestles against demonic spirits. Worldly people wrestles against God, his rules and foundations that was set. I'll simplify the statement, children of the spirit wrestles against demonic spirits and powers, and children of the flesh wrestles against God and his authority. I believed that was one of the issues within Jacob he was struggling with, which he had to wrestle. Unlike his fathers, Jacob always outsmarted the next person and did things his way in control, then to yield whole heartedly to God. Jacob's physical and spiritual wrestling is described in the bible. The bible states, "And Jacob was left alone; and there he wrestled a man with him until the breaking of the day. And when he saw that he prevailed not against him, he touched the hollow of his thigh; and the hollow of

Jacob's thigh was out of joint, as he wrestled with him" (Genesis. 32:24-25). That was a physical description of what was going on spiritually.

Here's an example of a spiritual wrestling Jacob was dealing with. Jacob had a dream regarding a ladder that went from earth to heaven and God's angels was going up and down on it. The Lord stood above the ladder and made it known to Jacob who he was. God stated to Jacob, "And behold, I am with thee, and will keep thee in all places whither thou goest, and will bring thee again into this land; for I will not leave thee until I have done that which I have spoken to thee of" (Genesis. 28:15). After the Lord made his statement this is what Jacob said, "And Jacob vowed a vow, saying, If God will be with me, and will keep me in this way that I go, and will give me bread to eat, and rainment to put on, so that I come again to my father's house in peace: then shall the Lord be my god: (Genesis. 28:20-21). See how Jacob gave God all these stipulations and said, "then shall the Lord be my God", remind me of us and what we do with God. We have the kind of mentality towards God, "If you do this for me then I will…." and that's a part of spiritual wrestling.

God had laid down the law concerning this matter regarding homosexuality. God stated, "Thou shalt not lie with mankind, as with womankind it is abomination" (Leviticus 18:22). Man comes up with ways or reasons to justify partaking in this action, this is also spiritual wrestling. Someone set the rules and you decide to rebel and try to justify why you shouldn't be in violation. Imagine someone coming into your house and doing exactly that, how would you feel? Contrary to the structural format I have laid out in the prior chapters, I am going to do this chapter differently.

RESEARCH STUDIES REGARDING HOMOSEXUALITY

Concerning microchimerism, the effects it has on women with male DNA in their brain and blood tissue, it can have the same effect in homosexual males. I'm not regarding the percentage when involving a male fetus since males cannot become pregnant. Researchers looked at the part of the brain that's associated with emotions and found that straight women and homosexual men have the same connection between the brain regions associated with anxiety and mood disorders. A verse proving its possibility, "He that hath no rule over his own spirit is like a city that broken down, and without walls" (Proverbs. 25:28). Let's say a young boy who was a raped or molestation victim, the offender soul (along with the demons he has) will began to take ownership over the young guy's house. It's just like when a city or land has been taking over by enemies in a battle and after they kill all the soldiers they take the men, women and children as captives. Because of their defenses is down the spiritual demonic attack will be prevalent in their lives. Also, because of the male house have given residence to another male, they would begin to have the same reaction spiritually as women. The reason being due to another male DNA that has entered them. When the sperm enters them, it takes the same effect as it does with women (except getting them pregnant), going through their body, blood, and brain tissues.

HOMOSEXUALITY ISN'T ALL SWEET, IT'S MASCULINE BRUTALITY

An example from Jasher, "And by desire of the four judges the people of Sodom and Gomorrah had bed erected in the streets of the cities, and if a man came to these places they laid hold of him to one of their beds, and by force made him to lie in them. And as he lay down, three men would stand at his head and three at his feet, and measure him by the length of the bed, and if the man was less than the bed, these six men would stretch him at each end, and when he cried out to them they would not answer him. And if he was longer than the bed they would draw together the two sides of the bed at each end, until the man reached the gates of death. And if he continued to cry out to them, they would answer him, saying, thus shall it be done to a man that cometh into our land" (Jasher. 19:3-6). After reading that I wanted to know why there were beds in the middle of the cities?

I find it hard to believe that it was just used for measurements as some would like to debate. I believe it was used for more due to the passage I have mentioned earlier regarding having multiple partners. It even states in Genesis, "But before they lay down the men of the city, even the men of Sodom, compassed the house the house round, both old and young, all the people from every quarter: And they called unto Lot, and said unto him, where are the men which came unto us this night? Bring them out unto us, that we may know them" (Genesis. 19:4-5). If you were to continue to read that story verses 7 and 8 confirms that the situation was regarding sex, taking someone manhood.

It reminds me of what goes on in the prison system, where some predator prey on the weaker individuals to rape them. That is defiling the male, but it goes back even farther than that. During slavery times, not only was the women and children getting raped, but it was some of the most masculine men were also raped. This thing was called breaking in the buck. It was done to keep fear into the other slaves, just in case they wanted to get buck (and rebel) or run away.

I believe this was also done to alter out the man original DNA which came from his father and will continue through him. In the bible, the lineage goes through the father for example, the God of Abraham, Isaac, and Jacob. Also, the son carries the nationality for example, the twelve children of Israel represent a tribe, Esau, the father of the Edomites, Moab, the father of the Moabites etc… The bible also backs this statement, "And he said, when ye do the office of a midwife to the Hebrew women, and see them upon the stools; if it be a son then ye shall kill him: but if it be a daughter, then she shall live" (Exodus. 1:16). Why was it important to kill the sons? Because it will kill the race. Since they were not able to kill every male during slavery they would break in the buck. I believe it was an attempt that their DNA will mix with the slave. The slave wouldn't have a pure DNA to carry on his nationality. That attempt also reminds me of the eugenics program and abortion in our modern time.

THE CURSE OF CANAAN

When you read Leviticus the 18th chapter it goes into details of the abominations when it pertains of having sexual intercourse outside of God covenant. Because of the Canaanites practiced this wickedness frequently they had to be removed from off the land. The land they were living on became defiled because of their ill practices. They were spiritually making worship shrines at the place they did their wicked practices. Also, they were opening portals for demons to inhabit due to their practices where God wasn't receiving any of the glory. What the Canaanites were doing by nature (all the abominations of God) they were simultaneously living the curse that was placed on their father Canaan by his grandfather Noah.

The curse that was placed on Canaan was that he was to be a servant to his uncles Shem and Japheth. We know it wasn't only Canaan being a servant, but also Canaan's descendants to Shem and Japheth's descendants. This is how generational curses work. God states, "I will visit the iniquities of the parents upon the children to the 3rd or 4th generation" (emphasis added). A curse is a covenant that's made to keep whoever the curse was intended for or the person that came into an agreement with demons oppressed in all aspect throughout life. The wickedness that the Canaanites were doing was designed to keep them spiritually oppressed due to the curse from Noah. They were to be the tail instead of the head and beneath and not above.

While I was reading Leviticus the 18th chapter it became clear to how the curse was placed on Canaan. Starting at verse 6, "None of you shall approach to any that is near of kin to him, to uncover their nakedness: I am the Lord. The nakedness of thy father, or the nakedness of thy mother, shalt thou not uncover: she is thy mother; thou shalt not uncover her nakedness. The nakedness of thy father's wife shalt thou not uncover: it is thy father's nakedness" (Leviticus. 18:6-8). Some people that have touched on this topic claims that Ham (Noah's son) have slept with his mother or if Noah had another wife slept with her based off of verse 8. They use that as an origin to back up Nimrod marrying and sleeping with his mother and that way of life trickled down from Ham. I believe that the situation between Ham and Noah goes deeper than that.

Beginning at verse 7, it has made a distinction between the father and the mother. Wait a minute! I thought when the father cleaved unto the mother they became one and she became his nakedness. She does, but the word "or" in verse 7 makes a distinction regarding the father and the mother individually. In Genesis it states, "And he drank of the wine, and was drunken; and he was uncovered in his tent. And Ham, the father of Canaan, saw the nakedness of his father, and told his two brethren without" (Genesis. 9:21-22). In those two verses it was talking about Noah and his condition in the situation. I believe the word saw in Genesis is just like uncover in Leviticus. "And Noah awoke from his wine and knew what his younger son had done unto him" (Genesis. 9:24). Because Noah was drunk and passed out I'm pretty sure he didn't consent or agree with the wickedness that was done unto him, so it was like he was date rape. If Ham was playing peek-a-boo (and just looking) while his father was drunk, how would his father know what was done if Ham didn't touch (violate) him?

Since Ham was the one to offend Noah why was Canaan cursed and not Ham? The curse went after Ham's seed because he couldn't curse Ham directly. Because of Noah being violated and Ham cleaving unto him, any curse Noah would have directed towards Ham, he would also feel the effects of the curse also.

BREAKING DOWN THE SPIRITUAL EFFECT

Like what I have done in previous chapters breaking down a few verses to make my point, I am going to do the same with Romans 1 from 27 to 32.

Paul wrote, "And likewise also the men, leaving the natural use of the women, burned in their lust one toward another; men with men working that which is unseemly, and receiving in themselves that recompense of their error which was meet" (Romans. 1:27). This verse is obvious far as their attraction to the same sex, they completely left alone the opposite sex. What stood out to me regarding this verse was the last part where it states, "receiving in themselves that recompense". By doing what they want with body, they're going to reap the payment with it. At another former job, I had to transport this guy who looked young, but he had to go dialysis three days out of the week. It stunned me a bit because he was going to dialysis being young and noticing that it looked like his health was deteriorating rapidly by his skin. His color didn't look normal, looked like he recently got over the chicken pox and the scars were still there, and feet looked swollen and infected. One moment he was walking to the van and the next moment he couldn't; and had to be transported by a wheelchair. I wanted to know how could he be in such horrible condition. I believe I have received my answer when I had to drop him off home and some guy was waiting to assist him. Thinking nothing of it, I guessed the guy was either a roommate or a family member; until I noticed his ring on his ring finger. The guy who was waiting had a woman's diamond ring and the other guy (who I was transporting) had a band on. You guessed right, they were a couple and I believe God was showing me the manifestation of what happens when you live outside his word and justify yourself.

Continuing with what Paul stated, "And even as they did not like to retain God in their knowledge, God gave them over to a reprobate mind, to do those which are not convenient;" (Romans. 1:28). This verse points out the wrestling with God as I stated earlier in this chapter. Humans like to do what they want since they have the freedom to do so, instead of yielding to and following God. This came to a point while knowing God's word and struggling to yield to it, they would just flat out refuse to do it or even attempt to try. Doing that, they have become the epidemy of a carnal person.

As you see the spiritual wrestling starts off in the mind. Continuing, "Being filled with all unrighteousness, fornication, wickedness, covetousness, maliciousness; full of envy, murder, debate, deceit, malignity; whisperers, backbiters, haters of god, despiteful, proud, boasters, inventors of evil things, disobedient to parents, without understanding, covenant breakers, without natural affection, implacable, unmerciful:" (Romans. 1:29-31). Everything that I have just mentioned in Romans 1:29-31 are the spiritual effects (you can also say fruits) of homosexuality.

I know someone who possibly reading this and struggling with homosexuality would state "I have never murdered anyone". The statement can be true for you physically, but what about spiritually? John states, "Whoso hateth his brother is a murderer: and ye know that no murderer hath eternal life abiding in him" (John. 3:15).

Starting at verse 31 of Romans 1 states, "without understanding" that part got my attention I'm not only saying that because I'm writing this book. It's one thing using your body to satisfy your flesh not knowing the spiritual effect and the stronghold it creates. It's another thing justifying your situation and putting yourself in a position to teach others. I have to say it, I do not at all agree with minister or pastors who are homosexual because after what I have broken down, the bible says so. One of the spiritual effects is being without understanding, so how can they teach the word of God without understanding? Proverbs states, "Wisdom is the principal thing; therefore, get wisdom: And with all thy getting get understanding" (Proverbs. 4:7). Through thy precepts, I get understanding: Therefore, I hate every false way (Psalms. 119:104). In the lips of him that hath understanding wisdom is found…(Proverbs.10:13a). Paul states, "Whom we preach, warning every man and teaching every man in all wisdom; that we may present every man perfect in Christ Jesus: (Colossians. 1:28). With everything I have just presented you cannot do that without any understanding.

Another statement regarding the fruits of that spirit is being unmerciful. A perfect example, if someone were to speak out against their actions or the fact the law changing in their favor, they would try to put that person through the ringer to be frowned upon or even have prosecuted. Rather than forgiving or being merciful towards the person who did wrong by them.

Debate is another one that I have found interesting, because it can be used as a platform for justification. Pastor Darby in his video states, "Debates is rooted in the spirit of strife". I have seen a few videos of people preaching the gospel in the street and when a homosexual comes along, they always questioned their doctrine. If they are not questioning it, they will try to turn the crowd away from listening. If that fails, they will (in some cases) blatantly interrupt the teaching.

Proud (pride) is another fruit that manifest with that spirit and the proof is in their symbol (or flag). The rainbow was to symbolize the covenant that was made between God, man and the animals. God stated, "And I will establish my covenant with you; neither shall all flesh be cut off anymore by the waters of a flood; neither shall there anymore be a flood to destroy the earth. And God said, this is the token of the covenant which I make between me and you and everything creature that is with you, for perpetual generations: I do set my bow in the cloud, and it shall be for a token of a covenant between me and the earth" (Genesis. 9:11-13). The covenant was made due to Adam fall into sin, that man was going to be corrupt and he wouldn't just constantly destroy his creation. God also stated, "And the Lord smelled a sweet savor; and the Lord said in his heart, I will not again curse the ground anymore for man's sake; for the imagination of man's heart is evil from his youth; neither will I again smite anymore everything living, as I have done" (Genesis. 8:21). That verse also confirms how everything starts off in the mind and not casting things down that evil. So, when you see the flags or a parade, it is a mockery towards God. It's like stating, we can do what we want and cause of this covenant you made, you can't destroy us for it, a perfect example of spiritual wrestling.

    Last verse concerning Romans 1, "Who knowing the judgement of God that they which commit such things are worthy of death, not only do the same, but have pleasure in them that do them" (Romans. 1:32). That's crazy not only they know the consequences but also enjoys it without shame.

Chapter 6
Lesbianism:

Covenant from emotions?

    This situation is like a double whammy when it comes to wrestling spiritually. It's more to women than to exercise their flesh like homosexuality. They also want, what they will call equal rights. They want the same rights as a man (although God created them differently) and feels they're missing out if they don't receive it. They are feeling that way because of listening to the serpent; and, that goes far back as the beginning of time.

    In Genesis, it states, "And when the woman saw that the tree was good for food, and that it was pleasant to the eyes, and a tree to be desired to make one wise, she took of the fruit thereof, and did eat, and gave also unto her husband with her; and he did eat" (Genesis. 3:6). Although it gave a physical description, it explains a spiritual story as well. I believed when the serpent presented to Eve his offer, he was presenting to her his structured society system (which is his world). Everything that she saw was the lust of the flesh, lust of the eyes, and the pride of life (1 John. 2:16). In the order that God created was: God, Adam, and then her. In the serpent's offer she would have been the pioneer of it. After she ate

The Spiritual Effects of Sex

of the fruit she gave to her husband and he also ate, notice the reversal of the order. She was able to be the teacher to her husband, which gave her authority over him. In Job, it states, "For the ears trieth words, as the mouth tasteth meat" (Job. 34:3). That verse describes an example of eating spiritually.

Women are usually put in position where they wrestle spiritually as a part of nature or instinct. Leah and Rachel were both Jacob's wives, Jacob loved and wanted Rachel, but he was duped into getting Leah. Jacob had to work twice as hard to get Rachel, only to find out that she was barren. The Lord opened Leah wound because Jacob hated her compared to Rachel. Leah birthed four sons for Jacob. Rachel couldn't have any children then, so she gave her handmaid to her husband to have children (like a surrogate mother). Rachel states, "And Rachel said, with great wrestlings have I wrestled with my sister, and I have prevailed: and she called his name Naphtali" (Genesis. 30:8). This verse interested me because Rachel had done this spiritual wrestling when she was barren. It shows the measure women will go to when things don't naturally go their way (they'll find a way). It also reminds me of how two women that are a couple will adopt, find a surrogate mother, or conceive artificially.

When God created women, he created them uniquely and gave them an assignment only they can perfect. Why they have the need to want more or is never satisfied? The serpent is playing on their emotions and is the driving force behind them wanting more, and it's usually for his own agenda. I know you are asking by now after reading the previous chapters, how can two women cleave together to become one flesh when they both are receivers and not having the proper equipment to do so? I believe if they were to cleave to each other, it will have nothing to do with the physical action (like the other scenarios that DNA have proved). The cleaving process would be more spiritual with the assistance of demons. I know that's a very big hunch and I have to prove my point. Also, I will have to find out are two women, being joined into one illegally? Or, are the demons involved in the mischief (behind the scenes), playing mind games on women emotions and possibly joining themselves together? While, the women involved never cleave, but their emotions are strapped along for the ride.

RESEARCH REGARDING LESBIANISM

Researchers have done an MRI scan on men and women who were both hetero and homosexual and found while gay men and straight women had a larger right brain hemisphere, that the brains of straight men and lesbians were anatomically symmetrical. While looking at the amygdala, a part of the brain that's associated with emotions, not only they found that gay men and straight women had more connections in that area of the brain associated with anxiety and mood disorders but also lesbians and straight men have more connections in that part of the brain pertaining to fight or flight reactions. Why the differences? Scientist can't determine whether it's the exposure to hormones like testosterone in the womb. In conclusion, there isn't any legitimate evidence to state someone was born this way. I believe God doesn't make any mistakes. If he was a God that makes mistakes it would've shown in his other creations. Whether it was able to move around like people and animals or be still like grass, trees, and water. Because of the lack of mistakes that you see in his everyday creation, I doubt he will have a malfunction during the development process in the womb. Based on the research study, what I believe happened is that a masculine demonic spirit has took over a woman soul (which made her a lesbian) is manifesting.

The research study found connections between the opposite sex from the part of the brain that deals with emotions, which is part of your soul. We know the brain is an organ that associate with the mind, that we use to think. Jesus states, "Or else how can one enter into a strong man's house, and spoil his goods, except he first bind the strong man? And then he will spoil his house" (Matthew. 12:29). Who the strong man you might ask? In Proverbs, it tells you, "A wise man is strong; yea, a man of knowledge increaseth strength" (Proverbs. 24:5). Wise man and knowledge has to do with your thinking. Where do you think from? Your mind, which is associated with your brain, but as Proverbs. 23:7 states, "it's your heart" (not the literal heart). Based on the scriptures and the research study, that masculine demonic spirit made itself manifest in the brain (which is the organ for the mind). It is prevalent in the area which deals with emotions. Once that was capture it wasn't going to be long before it manifested itself to act out through the person (which is the will).

BREAKDOWN REGARDING LESBIANISM

"For this cause, God gave them up unto vile affections: for even their women did change the natural use into that which is against nature: (Romans. 1:26). In this verse for God to have given them up, they had to be rebellious far as his authority in their lives. Paul states, "Because that, when they knew God, they glorified him not as God, neither were thankful; but became vain in their imaginations, and their foolish heart was darkened" (Romans. 1:21). The part that says, "became vain in their imaginations" interest me because according to 2 Corinthains. 10:4 it explains that the weapons we must fight with are spiritual and mighty through God. The following verse gets specific regarding how to fight and one of the things it mentioned is "casting down imaginations". In Roman 1:21 it states they became vain, meaning, they let their imagination run wild without casting it down. Because of that, the spirit behind it becomes stronger in their lives. Also, regarding in that verse the phrase "their foolish heart" reminds me of proverbs. It states, "Foolishness is bound in the heart of a child; but the rod of correction shall drive it far from him" (Proverbs. 22:15). So, that means they have a mentality of a child. If that's the case, could that be the manifestation of them at one point being a victim (which I will get into my next chapter).

Is it possible for a woman to receive another woman's DNA? In one possibility, yes and that's through kissing. While kissing, bacteria, bodily fluids, and parts of their DNA genetic code swap between the two participants. Unlike microchimerism where DNA can be left in someone for decades, with kissing it only last on your lips for at least an hour. Also, in microchimerism they were only able to only detect the Y chromosomes, which usually comes from males. I couldn't find any scientific evidence of a woman that was able to leave her DNA into another woman. The reason being is women don't have any Y chromosomes like men that can be detected. Can the cleave process happen between two women? Unfortunately, no, so what's going on? I believe it's more of demons manipulating on emotions and possessing women.

The same effects or fruits of Romans. 1:29-31 that applies in homosexuals also applies in lesbians. After everything it mention and the bible states, "their foolish hearts were darkened" explains how engaging in lesbianism is a fast way to get demon possessed. When a woman is getting ready to or at that moment of climax, I believe that's when she spiritually opens up to receive. On the flip side I believe when men are at their climax point, they're release themselves spiritually. When the women (that are lesbians) are engaging in exercise their flesh and they're both are receivers, what spirit is going to be there when they open themselves up? My guess is the spirits that they have attached to one another.

Chapter 7
Pedophilia:

Preyed on a child, bound by a spirit

If you thought the last chapter blew you away, this is where things get a bit more interesting. Understanding how the cleaving process work from the beginning chapters. Also reviewing the scientific evidence presented based on different scenarios. Lastly, demons manifesting themselves when sexual encounters go off course. It has become a double whammy when it comes to this situation. When I have mentioned double whammy in the last chapter it was regarding my interpretation of spiritual wrestling.

The double whammy in this case pertains to the spiritual effect. Not only the cleaving process work when it involves the male counterpart releasing themselves physically and spiritually, and a female or a boy victim is on the receiving end. Also, in this situation the demons involved manifest in more ways than one. This is where the cleaving process interrupt (spiritually) and intersect (physically) with the development process in a child. When that happens, this is usually where strongholds are created. What makes it a stronghold in someone life is their mental development is capture while their physical development continues to grow. This is where a lot of times people mentally doesn't match their age and the age they act is most likely where they were captured.

THE SPIRIT BEHIND THE PREDATOR

One spirit behind the predator is usually covetous. I stated that because it's the root of lust. Paul clarified, "……. for I had not known lust, except the law had said, Thou shalt not covet" (Romans. 7:7). Also, control, manipulative, deceitful, and cunning. Those description reminds you of the serpent. They are not only passing off their DNA but, the spirits they have attached to them as well. Everything gets handed off to a child, who isn't fully developed and doesn't understand what's going on physically or spiritually. Unfortunately, they were signed up for a stronghold cycle and generational curse (if the crime occurred in house) that keeps going. That's how a lot of times the victims, victimizes others. They could operate in some of those spirts as a tool of defense, not to become vulnerable again.

At my former job I have dealt with guys who were mentally disabled. They have committed sexual acts against children and currently registered as sex offenders. Due to their mental disability there were able to avoid prison. What I have found to be interesting looking back from working there is that you were able to see that spirt operate through them. These guys as I mentioned earlier were mentally disabled they needed assistance with a lot of basic functions. Some of them couldn't count out their own money or take care of their hygiene without being reminded to do so. When it came to one of their victims or if they wanted to victimize somebody on their unit they would try to calculate many ways to make their desire possible. Sometimes I wondered how can someone that need help tying his shoe can elaborate on a plan like that?

One of the guy I used to work with confessed, "what he used to do to capture victims, is leave his apartment door open with cartoon shows loud on TV. He would also have a bowl of candy by his door to capture the kid's attention. It basically was a trick to lure the kids into his apartment. If a kid were to come in or somebody were to walk by the apartment door they would more than likely see him naked.

Another guy, due to his height (and stature), you would think he's a kid (even how he dresses), until you really notice the aging on his face. One of his confession he explained, "how he was able to get into a chuck e cheese ride with a random kid and was able to fondle the kid". By the grace of God, the child's parent came before anymore could take place. When confronted by the child's parent, he gave an excuse to why he was in there, claiming he's helping the child. When the child's parent mentions the police, he hopped away on his bike and fled from the scene.

The Spiritual Effects of Sex

Allister Crowley a known Satanist, who named himself the beast or 666 states, "when you mess with an innocent child that's one of the purest form of satanic worship". Doing pedophilia acts is one of the many ways of them receiving occult powers. When the child is a young male they believe that they receive dark astral powers

Jesus states, "And said, Verily I say unto you, except ye be converted, and become as little children, ye shall not enter into the kingdom of heaven" (Matthew. 18:3). When my pastor explained the verse pertaining to children, it stuck with me while he was preaching. He gave a few examples regarding children, and how observing them at times you can obtain wisdom. Children have outstanding faith and belief. That's why any make-believe story or tradition they will believe in it wholeheartedly. Anything a child may need or want, they have faith in their parents to provide it for them. A child can get into a scuffle with another child and go back to playing with that child like nothing happened. While my pastor was given those, few examples pertaining to children, I thought of the charity chapter in 1 Corinthians 13. It states, "Doth not behave itself unseemly, seeketh not her own, is not easily provoked, thinketh no evil;" (1 Corinthians. 13:5). At the end of that verse in the NASB version it says, "does not take into account a wrong suffered,". It convicted me; because, I can remember as a child not holding anything against someone, no matter the reason. The older I became, I find myself (whether legitimate reasons or not) holding grudges against someone who I felt have done me wrong.

From these two verses, I have mentioned, it led me to believe that children have natural charity along with faith and hope. As born-again believers, we must get back to that state in our lives. The corruption of this world has hardened us, while we were growing up. Charity verse continues, "Beareth all things, believeth all things, hopeth all things, endureth all things" (1 Corinthains. 13:7). These are extraordinary qualities that someone can have, let alone a child. Having those qualities as a child, they are being close to the kingdom than more people will ever be. What if that same child becomes a victim of something that they were in no way prepared for, how will that affect their development spiritually?

RESEARCH ON PEDOPHILIA

A research that was done at Germany's University of Kiel led by Jorge Ponseti states, "because pedophiles' brains are abnormally tuned to find young children attractive, means that it may be possible to diagnose pedophiles in the future before they are able to offend". Pedophiles have the same neurological reaction to images of those they find attractive just like normal people with ordinary sexual predilections. The different is with pedophiles their revelant cerebral (part of the brain) area become engaged (emotions) when they see children, as opposed to fellow adults.

This proved what I have mentioned earlier in the chapter regarding masturbation, and the restrictions on the individuals at my former job. The area of the brain, the prefrontal cortex, putamen, and nucleus caudatos become engaged whenever a person finds another attractive. That area of the brain is inverted (upside down) when it comes to pedophiles concerning this desire. The research paper explains: "The human brain contains networks that are tuned to face processing, and these networks appear to activate different processing streams of the reproductive domain selectively: nurturing processing in the case of child faces and sexual processing in the case of sexually preferred adult faces".

The study analyzed the MRI scans of 56 male participants, a group that included 13 homosexual pedophiles and 11 heterosexual pedophiles, exposing them to "high arousing" images of men, women, boys, and girls. Participants then ranked each photo for attractiveness, leading researchers to their conclusion that the brain network of pedophiles is activated by sexual immaturity.

Basically, they're using your brain (which is the organ used for your mind, will, and emotions (soul)) as an indicator to what you are attracted to. I believe they are testing, if your attractions are normal for a potential spouse or abnormal to something different. While they are testing, spiritually it will also indicate the demonic activity being prevalent in your brain. It's a test to see where the line is drawn for the test subject. Knowing the limitations, between caring for someone (like what a parent does) or a considerable age to establish a marital relationship. They have a set of pictures ranging from infants to adults for a test to detect their attraction level whether it's in normal or abnormal boundaries. The more the attraction would be in the abnormal range, the more prevalent is that demonic influence. The statement that was made regarding "high arousing" images left me with a question, where are they getting these photos to test with? I can understand (but don't agree with) X-rated photos of adults, because they just about everywhere. Then the question becomes, how where they able to get "high arousing" photos of children? It has you wondering regarding the testing done at some universities.

    Alfred Kinsey, (who the Kinsey institute is name after) during his research during the 40's and 50's paid pedophiles to rape children and timed it with a stop watch. Kinsey's research (which was funded by the Rockefeller Foundation) led him to draw the conclusion that children are "sexual beings" from birth. This flawed premise (based on research integrity) is what sexual educators in the world use to justify their mission. Below is chart description of Kinsey research.

AGE	NO. OF ORGASMS	TIME INVOLVED	AGE	NO. OF ORGASMS	TIME INVOLVED
5 mon.	3	?	11 yr.	11	1 hr.
11 mon.	10	1 hr.	11 yr.	19	1 hr.
11 mon.	14	38 min.	12 yr.	7	3 hr.
2 yr.	{ 7 { 11	9 min. 65 min.	12 yr.	{ 3 { 9	3 min. 2 hr.
2½ yr.	4	2 min.	12 yr.	12	2 hr.
4 yr.	6	5 min.	12 yr.	15	1 hr.
4 yr.	17	10 hr.	13 yr.	7	24 min.
4 yr.	26	24 hr.	13 yr.	8	2¼ hr.
7 yr.	7	3 hr.	13 yr.	9	8 hr.
8 yr.	8	2 hr.		{ 3 { 11 { 26	70 sec. 8 hr. 24 hr.
9 yr.	7	68 min.	13 yr.		
10 yr.	9	52 min.			
10 yr.	14	24 hr.	14 yr.	11	4 hr.

Table 34. Examples of multiple orgasm in pre-adolescent males
Some instances of higher frequencies.

Figure 4: The chart based on the research by Alfred Kinsey.

Chapter 8
The confusion of Bestiality:
God's not the author of it

My first precept, "Neither shalt thou lie with any beast to defile thyself therewith: neither shall any woman stand before a beast to lie down thereto: it is confusion" (Leviticus. 18:23). And the second precept, "For God is not the author of confusion, but of peace, as in all churches of the saints" (1 Corinthians. 14:33). I have brought out those two verses to show you where I came up with the title for this chapter. The focal point of both verses was the word confusion.

With that in mind I took the time to look up the definition. One definition states, lack of understanding; uncertainty, a situation of panic; a breakdown of order, a disorderly jumble. Another definition of the word states, the state of being bewildered or unclear in one's mind about something, the mistaking of one person or thing for another. The word origin is the Latin word "confundere" which is mingle together. When splitting the word apart, which is con and fusion, I looked up the definition for both.

The word Con as a verb, is persuade (someone) to do or believe something, typically by use of deception; and as a noun, an instance of deceiving or tricking someone. Also, Con can mean a disadvantage or an opposing side. The word fusion as a noun, is the process or result of joining two or more things together to form a single entity. Also, it is the process of causing a material or object to melt with intense heat; especially, as to join with another.

The cleaving process is a spiritual process where the two individuals become one flesh. What is going on spiritually when you are dealing with two distinct species (humans and animals)? The spirit of confusion. Now understanding that, let's learn the effects of it spiritually and since God's not the author of it, let's go to the origin of it.

One reason I know for sure why God isn't the author of it because he is a creator. When God created everything from the beginning he did it from scratch. He was not following anyone recipe or starting where someone else left off. Here's a perfect example, he created two distinct species uniquely in their own way. He created them with their own abilities. The spirit or author of confusion, is something that is not a creator. Since that spirit cannot start anything from scratch, it will use something that was already created. The created thing or being would be taken out of its original form along with another object, to come up with something else. Before a mingled creature appeared physically through DNA splicing, the mingled creature had to appear spiritually through the cleaving process. What led me to learn more about this is, I always wanted to know why some of the animals in Leviticus 11 were unclean to eat. Why were the amimals unclean when the heaven and the earth was created everything that was created was good, except for the tree of knowledge? What I do know, for the unclean animals to be mentioned in Leviticus, they had to have been saved from the flood. God told Noah during the flood, "Of every clean beast thou shalt take to thee by sevens, the male and female: and of beast that are not clean by two, the male and female" (Genesis. 7:2). Now the question becomes, how did the animals become unclean when everything was all good during creation? Was it through DNA splicing?

INTRODUCTION TO STRANGE FLESH

Paul wrote, "All flesh is not the same flesh: but there is one kind of flesh of men, another flesh of beasts, another of fishes, and another of birds" (1 Corinthains. 15:39). Looking at this verse and thinking of the definition pertaining to fusion you can understand why God made that commandment in his law. What's going on is you are making flesh that isn't the same become one flesh. Because of the differences of the flesh, that what's makes it strange when they interact. The introduction to strange flesh was first recorded in Genesis 6, when the sons of God went into the daughters of men. This is where glorified bodies mingled with earthly bodies. Also, they introduced to men how to mix DNA as recorded in the book of Enoch, which is verified by Jude. Enoch recorded, "And they began to sin against birds, and beast, and reptiles, and fish, and to devour one another's flesh and drink the blood" (Enoch. 7:5).

    A lot of people believe that the sons of God weren't the angels that rebelled and fell, but the sons of God were of the lineage of Adam through Seth. However, that theory was wrong. To prove their case, they even went far as to take the spiritual (heavenly) meeting that took place in Job and made it a carnal (natural) meeting. Presenting their case, "Now there was a day when the sons of God came to present themselves before the Lord, and Satan came also among them" (Job. 1:6). Another verse to verify, "Again there was a day when the sons of God came to present themselves before the Lord, and Satan came also among them to present himself before the Lord" (Job. 2:1). Their rebuttal to those events, that the sons of God were the children of Israel participating in the feast. It was the children of Israel presenting themselves before the Lord, through their offering. The scripture they used, "Seven days shalt thou keep a solemn feast unto the Lord thy God in the place which the Lord shall choose: because the Lord thy God shall bless thee in all thine increase, and in all the works of thine hands, therefore thou shalt surely rejoice. Three times in a year shall all thy males appear before the Lord thy God in the place which he shall choose; in the feast of unleavened bread, and in the feast of weeks, and in the feast of tabernacles: and they shall not appear before the Lord empty" (Deuteronomy. 16:15-16). This helps backs up their claim for as the sons of God, being the lineage of Seth and not the fallen angels.

Also, in Genesis 5 where it talks about Adams lineage, each person that was named, it stated, they begat sons and daughter. That would further include in their case, those being the sons of God that went into the daughter of men (Cain's lineage of daughters). Here's a verse to squash that argument, "And Adam lived and hundred and thirty years, and begat a son in his own likeness, after his image; and called his name Seth:" (Genesis. 5:3). This verse made a powerful statement that people had overlooked regarding this topic.

It stated, Adam made a son in his own likeness and image; which, changed the whole course regarding Seth lineage. I know some of you may want to know, how can Adam have his own likeness and Image, when he himself was made in the Image and likeness of God? Everything changed after Adam and Eve fell from grace, by eating from the tree of knowledge. Before their fall, Adam and Eve was living and walking in holiness being in the image and likeness of God, while physically living on earth. Since eating from the tree, they became the pioneers of disorder, chaos, confusion, along with everything else that is in our world (structure society system). Their mentality became carnal, along with good in it, which gives them authority over others due to manipulation. Adam started out as the epidemy of what we are striving to be as Christians while living on this earth. Adam eating of the fruit, after being taught by his wife, thought he was receiving Godhood on another level. In the end he ended up losing the glory he once had. Due to his fall, he started receiving carnally and losing spiritually. Because of that, he began to establish his own image and likeness. The bible states, "And the Lord God said, behold, the man is become as one of us, to know good and evil; and now, lest he put forth his hand, and take also of the tree of life, and eat and live forever:" (Genesis. 3:22). Everything that have been mentioned, there is no way the lineage of Seth can be the sons of God. Adam fell from God's grace and made his lineage after his own image and likeness.

CONTINUING AFTER THE FLOOD

Sodom and Gomorrah were known throughout the bible for their wickedness. I believe God titled it wickedness, because they had everything going on in that land. The book of Genesis recorded an attempted gang rape on the Angels at Lot's house, while they were spying on the land. In the book of Jasher, it recorded the beds in the middle of the cities. Also, the event they had four times a year where they swapped women and children. In Jasher 18:14, where the verse stated, "and some" would that also have meant men and animals? We know by Genesis, it meant men; but, is it possibly recorded regarding animals as well? Jude wrote, "Even as Sodom and Gomorrah, and the cities about them in like manner, giving themselves over to fornication, and going after strange flesh, are set forth for an example, suffering the vengeance of eternal fire" (Jude. 1:7). Based off that description, Sodom and Gomorrah had a lot of encounters of bestiality. If they were doing that to bring confusion, they also were mixing DNA between species. What made Sodom and Gomorrah so wicked was, during that civilization period, the people on the earth were uncovering some of the things that was destroyed by the flood and began to practice them. In some parts of the earth, also in some US states, it is legal to have relations with animals. Other parts of the US they consider it cruelty to animals, which carries a punishment.

RESEARCH REGARDING BESTIALITY

Bestiality have been given a modern name when it comes to someone addition to animals, it is called Zoophilia. The types of Zoophilia breaks down in different names, that involves several types of animals. They have scientific names for sexual activities with dogs, cats, horse, pigs, birds, dolphins, lizards, and even insects. The reason of this behavior for some people where due to their location (like a farm) and there was no other sexual outlet for them. On the other hand, some people choose to do it because that's their sexual preference. Part of the reason of it being their sexual preference was either their desire for affection, love for animals and possibly their sexual attraction towards them.

A study that was done by Dr. Hani Miletski surveyed 93 zoophilies (82 males and 11 females). 12 percent stated they had sex with animals because there were no human partners available; while, 7 percent stated because they were shy to have sex with humans. Regarding females zoophilies, the main reason why they had sex with animals was because they were attracted to the animal. Sixty-seven percent of the females tested, had love and affection for the animal, and insisted that the animal wanted to have sex with them. Most of Miletski's sample preferred sex with dogs (87% males; 100 females) and/or horses (81% males; 73% females). What I found was interesting, only 8 percent of the males wanted to stop having sex with animals while the females didn't. Studies published over the last 17 years, using non-clinical samples report most zoophiles do not appear to be suffering any significant clinical distress or impairment because of their behavior.

The last statement basically states, they haven't detected any mental condition in the participants due to their sexual engagement towards animals. Although there was no detection physically, I believe there's more that took place spiritually, based off just reading the study. The men in most case had sex with animal because there wasn't a mate around for them. That was the lustful spirit dwelling inside of them and is willing to do anything to reach its gratification. Their sexual desire became so strong they could no longer control it, which they ended up using an animal to fulfill it. In the women's case, it's different, because of the spirit behind neglect, depression and desperately desiring for affection. It makes them easy target spiritually because of their vulnerability. Because of the area of vulnerability, they ended up committing an abomination. All in hopes to fulfill their desire. I want to know, how can the women sense that the animal wants to have sex with them, when they can't even translate the animal's language? I ask because, I know a dog when it is trained, can understand your language. Some of the more expensive dogs from what I have heard can understand 3 languages at the same time. Without the dog acting out through movement, how can you understand what the dog is saying by just the bark?

Chapter 9
Necrophilia:
Joining to the dead

    The topic regarding necrophilia would consider to be a crazy topic. Majority of the people wouldn't imagine doing such a thing, but there are many people that will and have done it. Just like any other sexual fantasy that has a spiritual effect, this one is no different. I know the effect of it will bring you into bondage, perhaps on a deeper level. Necrophilia is considered a practice of devil worshipping. You are becoming one with an object, because the dead body no longer has a soul to function in the physical realm.

    The psalmist wrote, "the dead praise not the Lord, neither any that go down into silence" (Psalms. 115:17). This verse can go both way regarding physical and spiritual. The corpse in this case, can't physically praise the Lord due to the soul leaving the body. Hopefully, they were praising the Lord while they were living, because they will miss the opportunity of rejoicing and praising after death. Once you die in this realm, all that you could do or have done in this realm will stop.

In Leviticus, it states, "Neither shall he go into any dead body, nor defile himself for his father, or his mother;" (Leviticus. 21:11). You are being physically alive and sleeping with someone or something that is physically dead equals you are being joined as one and becoming spiritually dead.

DOES THE BIBLE EXPLAINS THIS EVENT?

Luke the disciple wrote, "And when he went forth to land, there met him out of the city a certain man, which had devils long time and ware no clothes, neither abide in any house, but in the tombs" (Luke. 8:27). This verse is interesting because of the physical and the spiritual meaning behind it. We know by reading the scripture, it talks about a man who was possessed and living in the tombs. Tombs in our modern day would be like a cemetery. This verse explains how he could've became possessed in the first place. It stated, that the man has met Jesus outside of the city, which would likely be the wilderness. I believe the wilderness biblically represent adjusting to transforming spiritually. The city to me, biblically represents man's ideal foundation of the world (structure society system), which would be referred as adjusting to carnality.

When he ran towards Jesus It was like a cry for help, because he felt trapped by the way of society. The statement regarding the man, "having devils long time" sums up a lot of issues within him. Any generational curses that was passed down from his family tree. If there were any openings that he made from messing with Satan's devices. Covenants or oaths that he had made, along with any sins he participated in.

Also, "he wore no clothes", not only states he was naked physically, but he also wasn't covered spiritually. Remember in chapter 3 concerning the queen of the coast article where she stated, "the ones that are naked without cloth are the ones who haven't accepted the Lord in their lives and are used to assist them in their wickedness".

The man could've been physically homeless by the description of the statement, "neither abode in any house". When interpreting that spiritually, I believe it referrers to what this book has been about these last 8 chapters, the spiritual effect of sex. I believe he didn't have a wife for his soul to reside in spiritually. Another possibility, he may not have had any parents. As it states in the bible, "Therefore, shall a man leave his father and mother, and cleave unto his wife: and they shall become one flesh" (Genesis. 2:24). The description that was giving states, he physically lived in the cemetery when it mentioned the tombs. Spiritually, I believe that it was possible for the guy to have cleaved his soul to a corpse. By him becoming one with an object (because the body no longer have life), his life began to reflect dead things. Reflection far as where the spiritually dead hangs out at. His life being at a standstill while everything is moving around him. Not able to think for himself and accept anything given to him. Spiritually sleep, caught up in the world society like it's his only reality.

    Solomon wrote, "For to him that is joined to all living there is hope: for a living dog is better than a dead lion. For the living know that they shall die: but the dead know not anything, neither have they anymore a reward; for the memory of them is forgotten. Also, their love and hatred and their envy, is now perished; neither have they anymore a portion forever in anything that is done under the sun" (Ecclesiastes. 9:4-6). Their body is no longer functional, and their emotions, which is usually manifested by their facial expression, is no longer visible for everyone else to see. I wanted to know why the examples, "living dog" and "dead lion" was used. I know the lion represents boldness, along as an alpha male, because of him being the king of the jungle. Dog usually represent everything that is defiled far as what it is and it actions. For example, "As a dog returns to his own vomit…", "give not that which is holy unto dogs", etc. Although both animals having distinctive characteristics concerning them, the value of them is important, whether being either alive or dead. The characteristics of a lion is more of a "stand up", while the dog is more of a "shady" individual. The lion and all the qualities about it, won't do you any good while dead. Because at that moment it can no longer develop and grow any further. The living dog, although have a "funny" characteristic, would still have an opportunity to change and continue to grow. Here's an example of a dog humbling itself and striving for change. Jesus stated, "It is not meet to take the children's bread, and to cast it to dogs". And she said, "Truth, Lord: yet the dogs eat of the crumbs which fall from the master table" (Matthew. 15:27). Because of the woman faith was so great, her daughter was made whole that very hour. The woman was compared to a dog because she wasn't from the tribe of Israel, but due to her faith she never gave up from trying to receive her breakthrough.

The psalmist wrote, "His breath goes forth, he returned to his earth; In that very day, his thoughts perish" (Psalms. 146:4). The soul goes to the next realm (either heaven or hell), while their body returns into the earth. In that moment, he loses all ability to operate in the physical realm.

RESEARCH ON NECROPHILIA

Dr. Stuart Bassman, a therapist who has treated necrophilies, say that most people having sex with corpses believe it is "innocent" and is "not hurting someone". Dr. Bassman also states, that people with these tendencies often have "feelings of abandonment" and that their cravings are often "activated by one major event". Dr. Bassman even compares necrophilia to pornography addiction, in that they both involve "imaginary fantasy relationships".

    When reading this statement regarding necrophilia, I see that it's more than just pleasing the flesh, it's the worshipping of self. The other party that is deceased is nothing more than an in adamant object, nothing more than a sex toy to them. The initiator has feelings of abandonment and have imagine this type of event in their fantasies. The enemy have constantly sowed thoughts in them until, that seed of thought develops into a tree. Necrophilia has been classified into three types: which are homicide, regular, and fantasy. One example, happens after the person murders another. Another example, is when someone encounters a dead person, which includes it being their occupation. The last example is, someone letting their imagination grow wild until they have to fulfill it. The motivation for engaging in this behavior is, most necrophilies desire to possess an unresisting and a non-rejecting partner. They want to be in complete control of the situation. They don't want anyone (or anything) that will put up a fight or have an opinion.

Chapter 10
Positions:
Antenna for possession

This topic was tough to do because I was struggling on whether to discuss it or not. It seems as no big deal because you might be switching positions to have better enjoyment in the bedroom. Here's the thing, your body is an electrical being, it receives and releases energy from your protons, neutron and electrons. Believe it or not you really are created in the image of God. According to Hebrews 12:29 when it says, "For our God is a consuming fire." The word that's describing God is the focal point, which is consuming. Consuming is not describing the fire itself, it's describing the energy behind it that's causing the fire to consume at a constant rate. There are four ways that electricity is stored in the earth, which is chemical, wind, solar, and hydroelectric. I have managed to find three examples that the bible gives how our body stores electricity. How electricity is stored in our body is the same way to how it is used in the earth which is by wind, solar, and hydroelectric.

In Genesis it states, "And the Lord God formed man from the dust of the ground, and breathed into his nostrils the breath of life; and man became a living soul" (Genesis. 2:7). This verse describes a process, using dirt (including all the elements that are within the dirt) and wind power while showing us balance between the spiritual and physical realm. From all the minerals and compound elements to make other minerals from the earth, man was formed with the materials from the earth. It also brings clarity to how our body is designed to go through trials and tribulation. Majority of the minerals and elements that comes from the earth usually goes through fire to inquire its highest value (worth). When the breath of life was breathed into man nostrils it shows how God created the body to operate using wind power. The respiratory system acts as wind turbines (that stores oxygen that keeps the body flowing electricity) while the air you breathe in is the wind power.

Jesus states, "The light of the body is the eye: if therefore thine eye be single, thy whole body shall be full of light. But if thine eye be evil, thy whole body shall be full of darkness. If therefore the light that is in thee be darkness, how great is that darkness! "(Matthew. 6:22-23). The light in this verse describes a source of energy which is solar power. Solar power is where energy is converted from sunlight into electricity.

Christ also stated, "He that believeth on me, as the scripture hath said, out of his belly shall flow rivers of living waters" (John. 7:36). I asked my self what did Jesus meant by living waters? I have received my answer comparing it to still water. In the pond, the water is still, it doesn't move, not productive just at a standstill. On the other hand, a river or a site like Niagara Falls the water is constantly moving. Because of the constant movement of the water, it has become an energy source that can be used to store electric, which is called hydroelectric.

I have given those brief description to explain how we as humans are electrical beings and how our God is a constant flow of energy and without him we are nothing, he is our everything. Remember in the story of Moses in the wilderness with the people and it was describing God's arrival to talk with Moses? It describes when he arrived as a pillar of smoke that got so thick where it covered up Moses, so the people couldn't see him. The smoke was describing the constant flow of energy, just like adding more wood to the fire and the smoke gets thicker.

Before I get to the core of the topic I have to explain how your body can become an antenna signal. Yoga is derived from a sankrit word "yuj" which means to unite or integrate. It also essentially means, "that which brings you into reality." I found that to be interesting because we are spiritual beings housed in a physical shell to navigate in this physical realm. Being brought into reality by Yoga description is acknowledging and connecting with the spiritual realm. There are four types of yoga which is Karma (body), Kriya (energy), Bhakti (emotions), and Gnana (mind). The four types of yoga I have mentioned each are ways to reach the ultimate, which is connection with the spirit realm and even possession. Also, they can be in perfect tune (on one accord) to work together. Many people use yoga as a form of exercise or stretching that helps keep them in shape. What most people don't know is each stretch, stance, or position is adjusting your antenna for the spirit realm.

What I believe on how all of this came about is this is one of the earliest warfare attack strategy from falling angels and demons against humans. When God created the earth, it was his physical replica of what is was like in the spirit realm. Paul letter to the Romans states, "For the invisible things of him from the creation of the world are clearly seen, being understood by the things that are made, even his eternal power and Godhead; so that they are without excuse:" (Romans. 1:20). Everything that was created on earth by God and how they functioned throughout the earth had a purpose physically and spiritually of understanding God. Here's the dilemma, everything that was created in the spiritual realm didn't have a replica of it on earth, that was because they were to be used in the earth for a different purpose, in some cases prophecy. Here's an example of an animals created differently in the spirit realm that didn't rebelled against God. In Daniel chapter 7, in his dream that he wrote, he describes 4 beasts coming from the sea each being different from each other and he described how each of them looked. How Daniel described the 4 beasts wasn't like anything you have seen on earth physically, but that was how they look in the spiritual realm. Daniel goes to interpret what the beast means in the physical, "These great beasts, which are four, are four kings are four kings which shall arise out of the earth" (Daniel. 7:17).

    Now you know that the mingled creatures that was created in the spiritual realm were supposed to represent kingdoms, governmental system, and future events that take place throughout the earth. Some of the mingled creatures that was created in the spiritual realm along with Lucifer didn't see a replica of themselves in the earth and may have felt some type of way which had led to their rebellion. So, when the rebellious angels left their first estate (heaven, emphasis from Jude. 1:6) they began to make war against God and his creation to make replicas of themselves on earth that God created. What they have done first was sleep with women (daughter of men) to make offspring. Next, they taught men to mix DNA between distinct species, so they can make offspring. Last, they were sowing their image into the heart of man (which is called imagination) so they can make graven images of them through sculptures, paintings, writings, etc. When God had begun to flood the earth due to corruption of man (mingled DNA), his continuous evil imagination (how some images were made), and the offspring of the rebellious angels. The only thing that was left on the earth (besides everything that was in the ark) were the spirits of the offspring because they didn't have an afterlife destination to go due to being offspring from two different realms the physical and the spiritual.

The Spiritual Effects of Sex

I had to give a little background to show where I believe spiritually how yoga was formed. Due to the offspring spirit of all sorts being created on earth in the physical realm gives them a license based of the individual agreement to inhabit them. This is where I believe yoga comes in, if an individual being and electric being made to receive signal by them exposing their body to different postures is agreeing to receive that spirit that is in tune with that posture.

Yoga has poses that are called the cobra, pigeon, dog, crow, and frog. These I believe tap into those animal's spirit or demons masquerading as those animals. When I see people getting spirits casts out of them some of them turn into animals like a snake and I wondered, how did a snake spirit get into an individual? Taking it a step further in Hindu (they claim Yoga is not a part of that) they channel spirits by breathing at a pace like a dog would.

Yoga also have poses for objects that doesn't physically moves like the tree, plank, bridge, mountain, chair, wheel, and plow. Although these objects don't move physically they serves a purpose spiritually. Trees in the bible represent the spiritual body of an individual. Although there are many types of trees in the world but the difference between them all our two things if that tree bears any fruit or not. In Judges chapter 9 it describes trees wanting to have a king over them, so they asked an olive tree, fig tree, and then a vine. All of them refused because the fruit that they beared brings glory unto God and to give that up to be promoted over men is ridiculous. When they asked the bramble tree to be king over them the bramble tree took their offer and told them to put their trust in him. I wanted to know why the bramble wanted to be promoted? When I seen why it was called a bramble tree it made sense. A bramble tree is called that because it's a tree that bears fruit while having thorns (like blackberry and raspberry). In Matthew Jesus states that thorns represent the cares of this world where the seed had been choked up and became unfruitful. So, the promotion for the bramble tree meant a lot to him based on how he views the world and the wealth that's in it.

After receiving a little understanding how things work you may be asking, what does this have to do with sex? Now let's begin. The same culture that originated in India that have introduced you to yoga have also brought you Kamasutra. Kama, which is one of the four goals of Hindu life, means desire (includes sexual desire) and sutra means the formula that holds it together. Basically, it's a formula on mastering and fulfilling lust. From what I have explained earlier in the book lust (desire) is rooted from covetous (Romans. 7:7).

I have explained throughout the book how engaging in intercourse is designed to open you up to the spiritual realm. By doing that the evidence has been manifested through scientific studies throughout the world. I believe certain positions in kamasutra (just like in

Yoga) can channel specific spirits regarding that position through your electrical antenna.

Animal style, which is commonly known as "doggy style" but all animal that walk on all fours use the same position. You notice the women that like that position wants a man that's an alpha or a leader of the pack. Nothing wrong with that especially if you want to feel secure and protected. On the flipside the man that got you hooked by that position usually mistreat you or dog you just like how it's done with the female in the animal world.

Froggy style looks like "doggy style" I believe in that position when you are channeling the frog spirit you are playing the game. The worldly game, men and woman jumping from one lily pad to another.

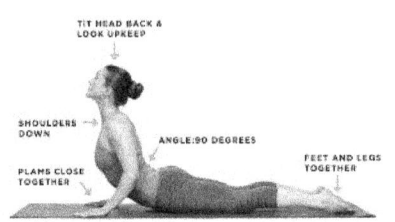 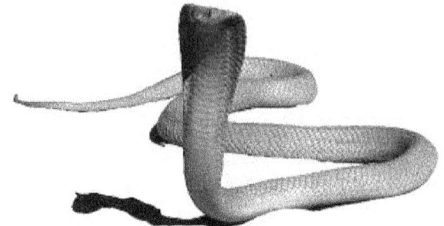

Cobra positions

Dog Position

Frog Position

THANK YOUS

This book was made to show what is done out of pleasure can affect us not only physically, but spiritually as well. In some cases, you can possibly catch a disease where it can destroy your physical body. You can also be bound and tormented in sin spiritually due to you thinking naturally. Thank you for your support and taking the time out to read this book. I also want to thank the Pastors (Damon Fulton) & (Stephen Darby) for sowing the word, which was used to further assist me in this book. Also, my wife (Shirlonda Cash) and my family (Parents, kids, and extended) for supporting me in stepping out in faith and completing this book. This book is dedicated to everyone who wants to break strongholds in their life after receiving more information regarding their mistakes out of their foolish decision. Those who haven't made any foolish decision this book is to further equip you with information not to fall into the same mistake as many of us who has.

www.ingramcontent.com/pod-product-compliance
Lightning Source LLC
Chambersburg PA
CBHW032045040426
42449CB00007B/989